MW01068103

1

Keep Your Peace On

ISBN-10: 1539008436
ISBN-13: 978-1539008439

For Worldwide Distribution, Printed in the U.S.A.

Keep Your Peace On

Limiting Strife in your Life

Nelson L. Schuman

Dedication

To everyone in the world who has lived out of fear, torment, control, or depression and has never known what it is like to live a peaceful strife-free life every day.

Endorsements

"Nelson has truly had to keep his peace on in the midst of a hurricane. Out of experiencing tremendous tribulations has come an extreme anointing for teaching others how to stay at peace and out of strife."

Tim Brown – Sr. Pastor, New Life Assembly of God,

Noblesville, IN

"To limit strife, you must be a great lover of Christ. Nelson has written a book that will guide you in loving and serving in joy, not in selfish gain through striving. The results produce contentment and peace in your life.

Owen Mason – Lead Pastor, Church Alive,

Lafayette, IN

"A servant of the Lord must not strive. Keep Your Peace On is a must read for those Christians who strive to live in peace. Nelson exposes how the enemy causes people to lose their peace and then lays out how to keep your peace on every day for the rest of your life."

David Natali – Sr. Pastor, Turning Point Ministries,

Carmel, IN

Testimonies

"Keep Your Peace On is a book that everyone needs to read because there is so much strife in the world and the enemy is affecting more people today than ever. If more people walked in the peace of Christ all of the time, this world would be a much calmer and more loving place."

"I grew up with no peace in my home as my father was an orphan and my mother had a monster for a father. Strife was an everyday norm and verbal assaults were expected. I have never known peace in my life after several failed marriages and finally now know that it was the enemy in me that I partnered with which robbed me of everything good. Thank you for helping me get my peace back."

"I have been married for fifteen years and have three children. I could not understand how to stay in peace because the enemy kept telling me that my husband was bad and I believed what I heard. After reading your book I realized that it was the enemy all the time so I commanded him to go and then I kept my peace on after that."

"I am a man who is 50 years old. I grew up not knowing my authority in Christ so was always afraid that I would get sick and die early. Every year I would get sick and then the enemy would tell me I was going to die. Now that I have read Keep Your Peace On - I have no fear or worries because I recognize that it is the enemy. I also used to complain all the time when I drove my car when other cars would slow me down or cut me off – but now I say nothing and remain in peace. Thank you!"

"My grandmother and mother were always worried about the future and how bad things could happen and then they normally would happen. This carried down the line to me, and I was extremely worried about my life and my children and then bad things would inevitably happen to me. After reading Keep Your Peace On I realized that the enemy is the enemy and when he whispers to me I tell him to go to Hell and remain in peace. I also received my prayer language and when I pray in it the fear leaves me instantly"

"I never met anyone who was not afraid of something in their life until I read your book and learned you could be free from all enemy attacks. That was such an amazing revelation to me that someone could stay in peace in the middle of such extreme dysfunction and trauma. Love it!"

"My family was wealthy and we never needed money for any of our desires. But none of us ever were peaceful as there was an unhealthy greed that was prevalent throughout. I became a Christian later but never experienced peace on a daily basis because of what was programmed into me by my family. Thanks for teaching me about demonic spirits and how they affect a person."

"All I ever knew growing up was strife and hatred. I never knew any other families could be loving like Christ. After reading your book and learning how to effectively command the voices to go from me, I now live in total peace for the first time. Thank you."

"If ever there was a time for this message it is now. More than ever the world is in so much strife and fighting and those who call themselves Christians are not much different than the world. It is time for peace and to walk in it every day."

"The church needs to rise up from the pulpit and explain the tactics of the enemy and how he whispers to the people to cause all strife. Keep Your Peace On is a timely word for this season and exposes what the enemy does not want you to know. Read it and do it."

"I never thought about where my thoughts came from as I assumed they all came from me. But after I read your book I began to start paying attention more and sure enough, many were from the enemy. It was an amazing revelation for me to catch myself dwelling on the thoughts and then taking them as mine and then bad things would happen after. Thanks so much!"

"Walking in peace every day was such a foreign concept for me to wrap my brain around. Thank you so much for putting this in the proper perspective so that I could understand what the enemy does and how to live in peace every day."

Acknowledgements

I want to thank all those in my life who have helped encourage me to press inward, onward, and upward in Christ. Out of the extreme tribulation developed an extreme anointing with which now the Lord is helping to set the captives free. Without my closest friends supporting me and being there when I needed someone, I do not know what I would have done to get to the other side of my destiny in the Lord. I love you all!

I want to especially thank all of my family and friends who the Lord has brought into my life who truly love me unconditionally and know my heart and compassion to help people with all I am capable of through Christ to live a life aligned with the power and love of the Lord. You are all awesome and I love you for your support and dedication:

(Aggie, Alan, April, Ashley, Austin, Becca, Bill, Bob, Brandon, Brian, C, Carrie, Cassia, Cindy, Charles, Chris, Chuck, Courtney, Crystle, David, Dawn, Deborah, Dianna, Duane, Elaine, Erin, Garry, George, Gina, Hannah, Keith, James, Jan, Jana, Jenny, Jess, Jessica, Joe, John, Jordan, Judy, Julie, Larry, Luke, Marshall, Marvin, Megan, Michael, Michelle, Misty, Neil, Nick, Nova, Owen, Patti, Patty, Paul, Phil, Priscilla, Randy, Remon, Robia, Ron, Scot, Sharell, Stephanie, Steve, Sue, Taylor, Tiffany, Tina, Todd, Trond, Tyler, and Tim)

TABLE OF CONTENTS

Introduction   19

Chapter 1 Our World of Chaos   25

Chapter 2 The Enemy is the enemy   39

Chapter 3 We are Not of this World   49

Chapter 4 Don't Look Upon Your Circumstances   55

Chapter 5 Be Like Christ   69

Chapter 6 Patience Is A Virtue   75

Chapter 7 It May Be Time To Part   83

Chapter 8 Love Me Forever Free   89

Chapter 9 I Will Never Strive   103

Chapter 10 Walking Out Your Peace   115

References   126

INTRODUCTION

I remember one evening, a week before Christmas in 2012, when I was flying back from a business trip to New Hampshire into New York City to catch a connecting flight back to Indianapolis. As my plane approached our initial descent, all I could see about 10,000 feet below me were lights and cars driving in every direction. I could sense in my spirit that most all of the people below had no peace in their lives and were just trying to survive another day of strife, fear, and exhaustion. My spirit was discerning that so many people in the city were worried about finances, spouses and relatives, concerned about their job situations, angry that others around them were getting in their way, and concerned about the upcoming holiday and having to endure words of strife from unloving cousins, grandparents, and siblings that they had not seen for months or years. It grieved my spirit because the whole reason for the season was to celebrate Christ being born to bring peace to a hurting world. We were to give gifts to each other to represent the three wise men who brought gifts to the newborn Savior, and we were to show the same love to all of those around us. Yet when I looked over what was a beautiful scene from up high of one of the largest cities in the world, my spirit could feel all of the pain, anguish, and lack of peace from everyone that was below on earth. It caused me to want to cry because so many people had been deceived by the enemy and tricked into turning what was to be a special remembrance of the greatest day this earth has ever seen into a season of greed, selfishness, and angst. On my plane flying with me, I could sense so many people who felt tension, fear, and lack of peace who were just sitting there suspended in mid-air as if they were inside of a slingshot getting ready to be launched at 100 mph into the airport and then out to their cars to fight traffic to a strife-filled, hostile home. Then the Lord spoke to me and said "My son, please tell My people that I love them and that nothing in this world is worth losing your peace over."

I think back to my life when I was growing up on a 160 acre farm in northern Indiana. The evenings we enjoyed consisted of peace, which I felt most of the time but now realize I took for granted. I never comprehended that other families in the world had parents that could barrage them with verbal assaults, constantly tearing their self-esteem apart. Now, decades later, I see the results of people's lives who had a different upbringing than myself who visit my Healing Rooms that now suffered from high blood pressure, heart disease, emotional dysfunction of fear, anger, depression, and extreme controlling and manipulation of their loved ones. Brothers and sisters would berate one another every day, put their siblings down, cause pain in their hearts, and develop anger inside that would eventually cause physical pain in their bodies for years to come. I could not even imagine that a family would behave like that as I'd never grown up with it and we genuinely loved each other and wanted each person to do their best and succeed. Did we have some disagreements or arguments at times in our lives? Yes, we did – but it seemed mostly civil to me compared to some of the stories of which I had heard of in other families. My mother and father did their fair share of arguing with one another as my father wanted to farm and my mother wanted a nicer home, but funds were limited. My siblings and I never complained about not having enough things. I always felt loved from both my parents as my dad came to most all of my basketball games and helped me with my homework if I had any questions. My mom encouraged my faith and prayed for me every day and they both attended church with my siblings and me on a regular basis. Their overall desire was to help their children do well in school and then see them each go on to college and live well-adjusted lives to love on other people.

We also never worried or feared over our health or dying of a disease or someone being tempted to take illegal drugs or drink alcohol in excess or commit any crimes. We did not have much money left over each month and could not afford a lot of new clothes, but we loved each other for the most part and treated each other with respect which is paramount to a family's well-being. If you could not love each other, then what kind of family would you have?

My world expanded after I began college at Purdue University in West Lafayette, IN and I got my first job selling software to banks with a company headquartered in St. Cloud, MN named Bankers Systems. I worked from an office that was located in my home in central Indiana and began to travel for the first time to other cities in other states. I was introduced to a broader spectrum of people as I traveled who did not experience as much peace as I did when I grew up. Some of them treated people disrespectfully and harshly, and were very selfish and not godly. Some drank alcohol in excess and were tempted sexually to do things they should not have done. I began to meet more and more people who did not know peace and made decisions based on their flesh that caused them more and more stress in life and led them away from peace.

Eventually in my own life, the enemy hurt one of my children and I had to start dealing with strife in my own family that was extremely hard to live with on a day to day basis. Verbal exchanges were not always respectful with strife between my children and spousal arguments that developed and increased. The stress and quarreling grew over time and unfortunately, divorce ensued that I could not stop nor reverse despite trying as best I could and spending thousands of dollars to no avail. My world rapidly developed into strife becoming the norm on a daily basis instead of the exception. My business career was still thriving financially for me, but I would have given anything to be able to have just a little peace in my life. All I knew at this point was tears and a tremendous helpless feeling to try to correct the dysfunction that was beginning to occur in my family while feeling the enemy was mocking me the entire time. I began to learn that without peace it does not matter how much money I could make as it could not be bought. Trusting in money and a huge retirement account was not worth it anymore because I wanted my children to make godly decisions in their lives, but I could no longer stop what the enemy was doing to them. I could feel that my health was being impacted because I could not sleep well at night as I would worry about what would happen to my children and my spouse if things continued to go the way they were going. Having to endure a divorce that I could not stop caused me to feel helpless and depressed as I was unable to correct what I could see was happening to my children. Watching my children become impacted in ways that I could not control was completely depressing and frustrating in every way imaginable; if I could have spent my entire retirement fund to save them from making decisions that hurt them, I would have. I was at the lowest point of my life, or so I thought, and could not see any light at the end of the tunnel.

What was happening to me was that the Lord was allowing me to experience an extremely challenging situation in order to prepare me for the real challenge that was in store later. My next challenge was immeasurably harder than my current situation. When I remarried a new woman and took on a couple of step-children, I had to deal with the enemy on an entirely new level. What I did not realize then was that the Lord was actually taking me into extreme circumstances and tribulations which would prepare me for my ultimate destiny. The Lord was taking me into a season of life to have me suffer for Christ so that I could eventually help thousands and thousands of others throughout the world who were in pain from the enemy. He wanted me to know what it was like for others in order to give them hope in their own lives and to ultimately be delivered from the enemy as I would reveal his tactics so that they could experience peace. The Lord said that it all was going to be worth it in the end, although the pain of enduring the many years of that season made it hard to see the end result on most days. Everything in me wanted to walk away and halt all of the strife and dysfunction, but something inside my spirit knew that other people were counting on me not giving up and that I had to endure it to the end to bring about the greater freedom in others' lives.

Now I can look back and see that the trials that the Lord had me endure were absolutely worth it in the end as I have learned so much to enable me to see what other families have to go through, and it breaks my heart because I know much of their pain. It has also allowed me to speak from a position of authority and experience when it comes to enduring the same things that befall most families in this world because I'm able to relate to their situations in a tangible way. My message to those who I speak to around the world is that if I could endure the extreme challenges and enemy attacks through people in my life and get to the other side, then so can you but only if you do not give up before completion. Although trials and tribulations are never fun to have to endure, they have a positive result if we persevere through the tests to allow us to become more like Christ. If we can understand that the more extreme the tribulation we endure, it will ultimately allow us to walk in an extreme anointing of the Lord and we will mature in our Christian walk to impact countless lives. Complaining about our situation does nothing but hurt the person's spirit that has to listen to it and keeps us from progressing into the Lord's future destiny for us.

Keeping our peace on is a must if we are ever going to develop a more Christ-like identity and grow in the Lord to impact the lives of others in a powerful way. Is it hard to live in peace with someone that constantly barrages you verbally day in and day out year after year? Of course, but we must do our part not to spew words out of our mouths that contaminate all those around us and give the enemy access to hurt us in ways that many have no idea. Life and death is in the power of your tongue and you will have whatever you speak. Speak negativity, fear, defeat or anger, and you will not see the fruit of your labor and not be able to help others that are suffering around the world. So speak life and live in peace and watch amazing things happen all around you!

CHAPTER 1

Our World of Chaos

The definition of peace is: freedom from disturbance; quiet and tranquility, calm, restfulness, privacy, solitude. Do you experience that in your life every day? Do you see much peace around the world? All one has to do today is turn on the news or read on the internet and there is chaos everywhere you look. The Middle East is always in conflict which really began the day that Abraham agreed to try to make offspring for himself instead of waiting for God's perfect plan to come to pass. For those of you that do not know the story, God told Abraham that he would have many descendants, but ten years after he was promised this – his wife Sarah still could not conceive a child. She was getting older and past the point of child bearing so chose to give her servant Hagar to Abraham, not outside the norm for that day, in order to allow him to have a child through her (Genesis 16:2).

Hagar ultimately conceived a child for Abraham, but then Sarah became jealous and despised her for bringing forth a son when she could not herself. So Hagar took the child (Ishmael) and ran to the wilderness for safety but the angel of the Lord told her to go back to Abraham and Sarah, so she did. Later, God fulfilled the promise He made to Abraham and Sarah when she gave birth to a son named Isaac when Abraham was almost 100 years old and she was 90. Ishmael was about 14 years old at the time of the birth of Isaac. There was more strife between Sarah, Hagar, and Ishmael, so Abraham finally had to send Hagar and Ishmael away when Isaac was almost three years old. The Lord then confirmed to Hagar that Ishmael would father a great nation when she was alone in the desert feeling like she wanted to die (Genesis 21:17-18). Ishmael became the father of twelve sons who were called princes and he lived to the age of 137. Ishmael ultimately birthed the nation of those in the Muslim faith today.

Isaac, however, was the chosen child that the Lord originally intended for Abraham and Sarah. He had favor upon him all of his days, as did his son Jacob and descendants after him. Ultimately Jesus Christ came from this lineage and came to give hope and bring love, joy, and peace into this world. All that have given their lives to Christ can inherit the blessings of becoming Christians today but due to the lack of faith that Abraham and Sarah had, there has been a constant lack of peace between the Muslim nation and Jewish people as well as Christians to this day. Many wars have been fought against the nation of Israel ever since.

Beyond just those that are Muslims, Jewish, and Christians, you can see the enemy at work throughout the entire world as so many people are angry, frustrated, jealous, fearful, controlling, manipulative, and sexually dysfunctional in every way. One country chooses to go to war against another country trying to control their people and take over. Evil is everywhere trying to steal peace from everyone. Countries such as Russia, Iraq, Iran, Turkey, etc. are looking to take over more territory and conquer more people and influence other nations instead of living in peace.

Beyond the nation versus nation comparison, let's think about what has been going on in the home of the brave and land of the so-called free. The United States has become anything but united as of late and so many people are not free from the enemy's attacks on their minds. Most people spew out feelings of anger, hatred, fear, and intolerance, taking offenses at the drop of a hat and offending people all day long. Every evil thought flows freely in their minds due to the enemy planting thoughts and causing behaviors that are unloving and painful. Think about how many people who are in such a state of fear and worry every day that they can barely function. They have to take medications to cope with the fear and then deal with side effects that cause them to want to take their own lives. Those that are regular church attenders and believers are in almost as much fear as those that do not attend church which should never be the case if they understood that they could walk in the same power and authority as Jesus Christ said we could and be free from all enemy attacks. This was unheard of 100 years ago as no one took any medication for anxiety issues back then and people, in general, were much calmer at that time than they are today. There were people who behaved in ways that were obviously driven by the enemy but the overall percentage of people with anxiety and fear issues were far less than today.

The enemy is having a field day with causing people to not go to God for their protection but to try to figure things out on their own and take matters into their own hands and trust in man instead of the Lord. We are an over-medicated world filled with under achieving believers in the church. If Jesus were to walk the earth today, He would have to retrain about 95% in the church as to what He meant when He said that we would do the same things that He did and even greater. The enemy has done a great job of creating fear, doubt, and doctrinal confusion within the church and it is time to get real and learn how to walk in the same boldness and power of the Lord.

27

Certain cities in the United States are under various enemy territorial control, and the enemy's presence can be felt more strongly on them as there are spiritual strongholds and principalities over their territories. On my business travels during my life, I have been to all 50 of the states in the U.S. and I have made many observations. Las Vegas has such a strong spirit of lust for sex, money, and control that whenever I went there on business my spirit would grieve for the people who lived there and I would feel sickened by the debauchery that was so blatant everywhere you looked. There were so many hurting people who were being used by the enemy that had no peace in their lives. Smoking, drinking alcohol to excess, and sex in your face wherever you went was literally unavoidable. You could not walk outside at night on their famous Strip without people shoving cards at you which showed nearly naked women, and ultimately many cards fell to the ground everywhere you walked. It felt to me like it was a modern day Sodom and Gomorrah. I also know several strong and powerful ministries that are there which are making headway, but the enemy does not want to give up ground easily and it is an uphill battle. You can hear so many people who travel out to Las Vegas as they talk on the plane about how excited they are in anticipation of hitting a jackpot or winning money or making a sexual connection lacking of total intimacy whatsoever. Then on the return flight back home, you can hear people talking about how much money they lost and how many are much more depressed and sad realizing that their flesh was unsatisfied and never could be. No peace was experienced and most are more disillusioned about their lives than ever or until they schedule their next trip back for another unfulfilled trip.

New Orleans has a strong feel of witchcraft as well as a lust for sex and alcohol. I know that not all the people are operating in that as there are many powerful Christians who are battling those territorial spirits to try to break them off the city, but it definitely is a challenging and arduous battle. I remember when I walked down the famed Bourbon Street well before Hurricane Katrina hit in 2005 and how I could feel such a sickening perversion of every type that I just wanted to run and hide as I had to shield my eyes and ears at the lewdness. Again, I felt like I was walking down the streets of Sodom and Gomorrah and was ready for the Lord to hail down fire and brimstone at any time if it were not for His grace and restraint.

I have only been to the city of Charleston, SC twice but both times I have felt a strong spirit of love, kindness, and purity. The people whom I have met there have largely exemplified the sense that I felt there as they seem to be very wholesome people who genuinely want to help others live pure lives and encourage people from a godly perspective. I live in Indianapolis and while many have a desire for things of the Lord and Holy Spirit, and helping people with their Hoosier hospitality, as they like to call it - there is also a strong spirit of Jezebel and Leviathan that is in the church trying to control and manipulate others and cause people to be prideful and come against the anointed and marriages. Godly people who are trying to do the Lord's work and get people delivered from enemy spirits and live pure before the Lord are thwarted by others who operate in Jezebel and Leviathan. My book *Restored to Freedom* has been making a positive dent in not only Indiana, but all over the United States and throughout the world. Unfortunately, there are millions and millions of people operating in those spirits worldwide and it is time to get clean and pure before the Lord in order to bring forth the greatest harvest this world has ever seen.

Then there is the city of Los Angeles. The name Los Angeles comes from the Spanish language meaning "The Angels" or commonly referred to as the "City of Angels." The original name is "El Pueblo de Nuestra Senora la Reina de los Angeles del Rio Porciuncula" which in English translates to "town of our lady the Queen of Angels of the River Porciuncula." I used to be employed by a company named Digital Insight, the largest internet banking company in the U.S from 2006 to 2012, that was based out of Calabasas and Westlake Village, CA - just northwest of LA (before being acquired by Intuit in early 2007 to become Intuit Financial Services before being sold off again). During that time, I traveled to

Los Angeles frequently on business – enough that I knew my way around parts of the area fairly well. Also, during 2008, my daughter Ashley got involved in a local acting agency in Indianapolis that had agents from Hollywood who would come to Indy to scout out new talent and one of them signed her to a contract. We made about 10 trips to LA for various auditions for commercials and TV shows. Since I traveled to LA so many times, I could sense in my spirit that while the enemy was very strong and prevalent in the various industries of media / entertainment (movies, TV, music, radio, etc.) which proliferated a lust for sex, money, and power - I could also sense that there was a remnant of people that were very godly that wanted the things of the Holy Spirit. Yes, the New Age mysticism was also prevalent but many of those people had a desire for the truth and were just searching and seeking for what was real and the enemy took them into New Age ideology.

I personally know a woman who was a very successful dancer and actress in Hollywood who was searching for truth and like so many, was introduced to the New Age movement. She still did not feel at peace in her spirit with their teachings because they taught that through your own self, you could help yourself. Unfortunately, she knew that since her own self had gotten her into a lack of peace, she correctly deduced that her 'self' could not get her back on the right track and out of the lack of peace that she was feeling every day.

So one day she cried out to the Lord on a freeway that if Jesus was the one true and only way to know God, then to make her aware in a real and tangible way that she would understand. Within seconds a group of bikers enveloped her car and on the back of their jackets it read "Hells Angels – We Ride for Jesus!" So funny how the Lord showed her in a real way that was unique to her that He knew would let her know that Jesus was the only way to Him. She and her husband now lead a church in Redondo Beach, CA called Deeper Life that teaches biblical truths at a very strong level where the Holy Spirit flows. They are now raising up people to come into their own Christ desired giftings and callings at a powerful level to affect people in their own sphere of influence in amazing ways.

There are many people who live in the LA area and southern California who are on fire for God and they are seeing tremendous miracles, signs, and wonders now. After all, that is where the great Azusa Street Holy Spirit outpouring began from 1906 to 1915. An African American preacher named William Seymour from Louisiana was one of the most influential individuals in the revival movement that grew into the Pentecostal and Charismatic movements. He left the South in the 1890's and traveled to places such as Memphis, TN and Indianapolis, IN to escape the horrible violence, hatred, and strife aimed at African Americans in the South during that period. Seymour moved to Indianapolis and attended the Simpson Chapel Methodist Episcopal Church which was where he became a born-again Christian. In 1906 Seymour joined a newly formed Bible school founded by Charles Parnham in Houston, TX. Parnham's teachings on the baptism of the Holy Spirit stuck with Seymour and influenced his later doctrine and theology. He developed a belief in praying in tongues as a confirmation of the gifts of the Holy Spirit.

Seymour moved to LA in February of 1906. On April 9, 1906 the Azusa Street Revival began. His emphasis on racial equality drew many historically disenfranchised people to the movement and due to his influence, the revival grew rapidly. Amazing physical miracles, dramatic worship services, speaking in tongues, and glory clouds of the presence of the Lord were evident throughout the nine years. Today, the revival was considered by historians to be the primary catalyst for the spread of Pentecostalism around the world in the 20th century. The City of Angels definitely was appropriately named.

Yet there are also many more people in LA who are desperate, depressed, angry, and who have given up on life and turned to drugs while desiring the peace that passes all understanding. I have a good friend that used to be one of them who was looking for fame in the 1970's and 80's as he was given a tremendous gift of singing. He was sucked into the enemy's promises of fame through sex, drugs, and rock-and-roll. Ultimately it almost cost him his life as he became homeless for almost ten years in LA. His testimony is powerful as he became so humbled and now has given his life completely to Christ, and the Lord is promoting him around the country as he is able to get others that are struggling with addictions to heroin and other drugs to become free through recognizing that there are spirits of Pharmakeia in the drugs. These spirits are real and keep people in bondage until they finally realize that they need a higher power of Jesus Christ to get true freedom and then to get their peace back that was stolen from them by the enemy. He is a true man of God who is eternally grateful to Jesus for changing his life and putting him on fire for the Lord and is a great ambassador for Christ.

There are so many in the world who are striving to achieve to move up in their careers believing that if they had more money that they would be able to have the peace that they are looking for. I know because I was one of them. At the apex of my financial services technology career, I had accumulated over $500k in my net worth. My goal was to get to $1 million by the time I was 40 years old and I was well on my way to getting there. I knew of so many around me in the corporate world who had a greedy spirit that wanted to make more and more money and acquire expensive things and that's just the way it was when you worked for corporate America. It is all about making more money, investing what you have to try to maximize future growth so that one day you could call it a life and then kick back, relax, travel the world, and try to get back the peace that you sacrificed your whole career for. Unfortunately, everyone that I met through business did not know peace, at all. They constantly tried to move up the corporate ladder, looking to connect with other people who could make them more money or try to gain favor from influential people to position themselves in the company. It was all about who they knew and not so much what they knew. In reality, it was all about striving upon striving to make things happen under their own strength and never experiencing the true inner peace that would satisfy them from the Lord. It was a great teaching point to me that

32

so many millions of people around the world thought that if only they had more money that they could enjoy their lives more but ultimately, they never found peace and the more money they had the less they trusted the Lord for their needs and so had no real relationship with Him. They lost their spouses and families because the enemy tricked them into believing a lie. The only true way to live a life full of peace was to trust in the Lord to provide for their needs and draw nearer to Him to direct them every day. They spent so much time trying to make more money for their companies but had no idea what it was like to rest in peace and let the Lord connect them supernaturally to His provision and having divine connections to others. So many called themselves "Christians" but had no idea what it was like to walk in the power and authority of Jesus Christ in their lives and hear His voice for direction and walk every day in peace.

On occasion I would be able to connect with someone at a more personal level and hear their real pain that they would hide from others because they knew they could trust me because I truly cared for them as a person and not just to leverage making money off of them. Many of them had children that were out of control and seeing false security in other things such as drinking, drugs, sex, over eating, piercings, and other vices from the enemy. Their children hung out with other children who were disillusioned by their parents that spent more time at work trying to make money than loving them unconditionally at home. They did not know what to do to fix their children but would pay any price in order to get positive results. Many of them had spouses that they were thinking of leaving because they'd lost their connections years ago, or they felt controlled and manipulated by their wives or husbands and were desperate to be able to live in true peace. Most all of them were desperate and hurting if they were to be honest, and I wanted to help them but was not quite operating full time in my ministry but knew the Lord was taking me into it at a very strong level. I had to be patient and wait for things to develop in my personal life and I began to see the ministry growing rapidly just a few years later.

I can sense that the entire world is screaming for peace but searching for it in all the wrong places. Instead of going to God and the Holy Spirit, people are turning to diversions such as golf, other sports, drinking, gambling, sex, drugs, over spending, avoiding confrontations that need to be discussed with their spouse, and not knowing how to deal with the pain they received from father wounds and/or mother wounds that have never been healed. Many know that something is not right within them but do not know what it is so they go to psychologists and psychiatrists and well-meaning counselors but most of them do not understand the demonic world and how to get people delivered from their demons. Instead of recognizing that these people are behaving in destructive ways due to demonic spirits whispering to them, keeping them controlled, manipulated, and hurting their relationships with others - they recommend medications which ultimately do nothing but cause them to feel like a zombie or worse. Trying to deal with a spiritual problem through head to head counsel instead of Holy Spirit led counsel does not get to the root of the issue and does not allow ultimate freedom and peace in someone's life. You simply cannot deal with getting tormenting spirits off of a person by not taking spiritual authority over them to command them to leave just like Jesus did and what we as Christians need to do.

Now let's ratchet this global problem of chaos down to the sphere of influence that surrounds your world, those people you see every day at work, church, and are in your family. How many people do you know on a regular basis that either have just a little peace or experience no peace at any time? When you go to your place of work, do you encounter people that are anxious, fearful, frustrated, and complain the majority of the time? How does that make you feel when you are around them for eight hours a day? Many people comment to me that they feel drained of life and have no energy for anything once they get home from a stress filled day at work as all they want to do is fall into bed and make it all go away. Then, what about those people that you chat with at church every Sunday and/or Wednesday? Most just talk at a high surface level such as, 'How's work?' (Ugh – they just had to remind you didn't they!) or 'How's the wife or husband or kids?' and again the typical response is 'fine' but if you press in to really find out how things are, many of the women will start to develop tears in their eyes because they are emotionally drained and feel no real love in their marriage and their children are not behaving or respectful like they desire. Men are better at covering up their true feelings but if they are totally honest, they are exhausted from their unfulfilling work, feel no true godly intimacy with their spouse, have no regular conversations with the Lord, and feel like a lone ranger every day as they are disconnected with their angry and disrespectful children.

So the common thing that all people are void of is true peace from the Lord. Part of their lack of peace is due to the decisions that they make every day and part of it is due to others around them who are being affected by the enemy who cause strife in their life. True peace allows a person to never partner with fear, worry, anger, frustration, and a myriad of other conditions on an everyday basis.

We cannot control how others behave towards us because that is their choice, so we need to learn how to bite our own tongues around them and to see them through the eyes of Christ (as discussed in detail through my *Loving Like Christ* book). Who we can control is our own self through our reactions when we are living our lives day to day. We can choose to not be affected by someone else by staying in peace instead of taking the bait of the enemy and responding in anger or having feelings of retribution.

There are several situations where it would be extremely hard to stay in peace. Consider if your spouse constantly gives you a verbal barrage that is like Satan himself speaking words directly to you that cut you to the core. Or, your children or step-children may disrespect you causing you to react to them out of anger, frustration, or exasperation. The strife can, however, be minimized if you choose to walk away to another room, go for a walk outside, or drive to a peaceful place for a time until you can get your peace back. So even though the world around us is exploding in chaos, we can still choose to stay in peace when we recognize that the enemy is the author of all strife. Never forget that the true enemy is *the* Enemy (Satan or His demons) and not our spouse, children, or others. When we can recognize that the enemy is working through them to cause them to come against us, then it is easier to pick up on it before we lose our peace. We can discern that someone is being affected and it is not who they really are.

In 2010 Snickers launched a new advertising campaign based on people turning into different people when they were hungry, aptly called "You're Not You When You're Hungry." The first commercial had Betty White appearing playing American football. The commercial shows a touch football game that, at first glance, appears to feature Betty White as a wide receiver trying to catch a pass but then getting taken down and tackled in the mud by the opposing team's player. The team that Betty is playing against calls her "Mike" and offers her a Snickers bar saying that he is not playing like he normally would. After Betty takes a bite of the candy bar, she instantly transforms into a young man whose name is Mike and is now ready to get back and play the game as he normally would be able to. The commercial ends with a quick appearance by Abe Vigoda, who also gets tackled to the ground in a rather brutal fashion. This is the exact same reality that happens every day in society when the enemy whispers to someone to get them to do what they want. They become this hard-to-get-along-with person who they are not unless they are under the influence of demonic spirits. They essentially become difficult to get along with because they have heard the enemy's voice for so long, but once they get the spirits removed that have been tormenting them, they become who they really are in Christ which is loving, kind, patient, and at peace.

Self-control is one of the fruits of the Spirit that so many Christians do not walk in every day (in addition to peace). I never knew what it truly was to walk in self-control until I started getting mentored by a very godly man who worked with me from Southern California named Chuck. He made me aware many times (so that I wouldn't forget), that I needed to memorize a scripture in my heart and then teach it to others since I would eventually be counseling and teaching hundreds and thousands around the world in the future. The scripture was 2 Timothy 2:23-26 NKJV "[23] But avoid foolish and ignorant disputes, knowing that they generate strife. [24] And a servant of the Lord must not quarrel but be gentle to all, able to teach, patient, [25] in humility correcting those who are in opposition, if God perhaps will grant them repentance, so that they may know the truth, [26] and that they may come to their senses and escape the snare of the devil, having been taken captive by him to do his will."

So even though we cannot stop someone from getting in our face, speaking out words that cut us to the core, growling, screaming, chasing us in our homes or hotels, or throwing knives or glasses at us, we can control how we react to them. We have control over our own words that come out of our mouths. Sometimes you just have to get alone and leave a volatile situation because the only response that could come out of your mouth would escalate the situation into World War III and nothing good will come after that. Have you ever tried arguing with someone that simply will not engage in the argument with you? It is quite difficult to have an argument by yourself when the other person says nothing back to you for more than a minute. You should try it the next time someone starts yelling at you. Just say nothing and as they continue to say horrible words to you after about a minute they may start thinking, "What is wrong with this person? Why are they not engaging with me?" Keeping your peace on may test you to the core of who you are as a person but with the help of the Holy Spirit, it is possible to do. No, it is not easy whatsoever to take verbal abuse over and over but what would Jesus do? Would he strive back with them? When you choose not to engage with the enemy in a verbal exchange of words, you cut off the fuel source. So I challenge you the next time someone starts to speak out words of anger, ridicule, and hatred, to 'just say no!' and disengage. Look at them with loving compassion as Christ would. It will definitely be a reaction that they are not expecting to receive.

The Lord knew ahead of time that the enemy would try to create as much strife as possible in this world, and especially in the lives of the Lord's people in order to cause them to partner with the enemy when he whispered things to them to act upon. He gave us basic instructions in His Word regarding how to behave and how to recognize demonic spirits that would speak to you trying to cause you to lose your peace and respond out of anger and frustration. Greater is He that is in you than he that is in the world. This world is a very harsh place to live but we are not of this world, are we? It is so important to recognize when the enemy tries to start strife with us so we can shut it down before we speak words from our mouth to hurt others. The next chapter will focus on who the real enemy is and how to identify him so that we can limit our responses to people to only words of love by seeing when a person is being used by the enemy.

Chapter 2

The Enemy is the enemy

A wife speaks a harsh word to her loving husband causing him to get hurt and take an offense for the rest of the evening. He then sleeps as far away from her in bed and the night is ruined causing both to have resentment and anger in their hearts as they think thoughts of hatred towards each other. A man speaks a mean word to his kind-hearted wife that causes her to cry and then eventually after ten years of harsh words, she has no love left in her broken heart for him and is talking to her girlfriends about divorcing him and they all are encouraging her to leave. A son is berated by his father over and over for his entire youth and then develops a hatred for him and wants nothing to do with him for the remainder of his life. A girl feels rejected by her father who works all the time and then when he is home, he wants to watch sports and relax without getting involved in her life. She later grows up with such pain that she takes it out on her husband by controlling, manipulating, and causing him not to want anything to do with her. Later, they separate after just six years and filing for divorce causes her to become even more hurt and angry at men, all because of an original wound in her heart caused by her daddy who was supposed to love, cherish, and protect her. A woman tells her sister-in-law that she needs to spend more of her time at church doing godly activities instead of doing so many non-church related events with her children. Her sister-in-law feels condemned and wants nothing to do with her or the church for the rest of her life.

What do all of these examples have to do with the enemy? They were all just words spoken out by people, correct? Wrong! The enemy first planted the thoughts in each of the perpetrators minds and after letting them ruminate for a few seconds or minutes – the people spoke out the words that were whispered to them. The results were all the same – causing the victim to hear the words and then their hearts were hurt in dramatic ways that many never recovered from. Some of the words caused permanent splits of divorce costing children a lifetime of pain and brokenness as even more damage was done to their innocent spirits for the rest of their lives. This is going on all over the world, every day, over and over and over, and people have no clue.

Unfortunately, every non-believer and also a large majority of the church, have NO idea that many of their thoughts come from demonic spirits. They whisper to them from the time they are young and throughout their lives trying to get them into anger, resentment, rejection, frustration, fear, etc. Our thoughts come from one of three places; our own mind, the enemy, or the Holy Spirit and God. It is up to the person to discern if the thought is coming from them, the enemy or the Holy Spirit. The enemy is extremely adept at speaking words that we think are coming from us but instead are coming from him. In fact, about 90% of what the enemy says to us is truth because if it was

40

more obvious, we would never buy into or believe it. It is that 10% of a lie that trips us up and can cause a lifetime of pain, anger, and sadness.

The following is an example. A husband and wife are driving to a wonderfully anointed Christian conference with several anointed speakers from around the world. About an hour into the drive, the wife receives a thought from the enemy. The thought is this: "Your step-daughter is such a beautiful girl. You are so lucky to have her as she wants you to be her mother since her own mother is such a mean woman. But so many boys also know how pretty she is and are trying to get her into a compromising position for selfish reasons. She has a couple of boys that you just cannot trust, and you'd better protect her from them. They may try to tempt her to hold a party at your house before you get back. You better have your son go check on her and see if she is having a party tonight. If only your husband would clamp down more on the freedom that she has – then you would not have to put up with watching her like a hawk. It is all your husband's fault – you need to tell him to tell her that she cannot go near your house or you will call the police and have them watch it for suspicious activity."

Then the wife speaks to her husband, "You need to tell your daughter she is not allowed to go to our house or I will call the police because she cannot be trusted by herself!" This causes the husband to feel hurt that his wife does not trust his loving daughter so he tells her that her own son has had relations with multiple girls at his house and she did nothing to stop him while his daughter has not had any relations with anyone. Then the next thing you know, the strife has escalated and there are elevated words that are being spoken back and forth. At one point, the wife asks him to stop the car so she can literally run away from him. Two hours later, the wife calms down which allows the husband to return to his drive to the conference but they are now stuck in the middle of horrible rush hour traffic in Chicago and it just started raining. He is now very upset with his wife because had she not spoken those harsh words to him about his daughter - the traffic issue would never have occurred and they would have already been at the conference near the airport instead of arriving hours later. For the rest of the conference, they are both mad at each other and do not hear a word of what was spoken by the anointed speakers. So the enemy won and the memory of that lost weekend was forever etched in the minds of the husband and wife. Later, both would bring it up to each other and this would then lead to causing more conflict and strife, all thanks to the enemy.

It is so important to recognize as early as you can when the enemy is speaking a thought to you in your mind and then say to yourself "Wait a minute – that thought I just had was from the enemy…so I am going to capture it and speak out 'I rebuke you and command that you be gone from me in Jesus name!' " So many people in the church today have no idea when the enemy is whispering to them thus causing them to do what he wants them to do instead of rejecting the thought and not speaking it out which gives it more life to hurt someone. Then, when they speak it out, it gives it much more strength and life to inject pain and anger to their intended target. We must develop our ability to discern what thoughts are from the enemy, what is from our self, and what is from the Holy Spirit. Any thought that is not uplifting and encouraging but instead has an ultimate destiny to hurt, cause strife, pain, rejection, control, or manipulation, etc. is from the enemy and needs to be commanded to go so you can come back into a more peaceful position in your life.

John 10:10 NKJV states "The thief (Satan) does not come except to steal, and to kill, and to destroy. I have come that they may have life, and that they may have it more abundantly." Satan wants to steal your peace and he does that in many ways. He causes people to speak out words that hurt us, and he whispers to you to cause you to speak out words to hurt others which ultimately creates strife between everyone.

It is so critical to discern that if you are ever not at peace, it is always the enemy. For example, if you are worried because you only have $10 left in your checking account and you do not get paid for two more weeks, then you are not trusting that the Lord will provide for you. This puts you on enemy territory and the Lord cannot provide for you because you are now living in fear. As soon as you realize you are worried, you need to recognize that it is a spirit of fear that was sent to harass you and cause you to speak out words such as "We won't be able to eat for the next two weeks! We have no money! We won't have any money for gas!" and then the enemy will be able to do what you have spoken because life and death is in the power of our tongues. Proverbs 18:21 NKJV "Death and life are in the power of the tongue, And those who love it will eat its fruit." So eat of peace and not fear, anger, or strife. Eat of love, joy, and freedom - not anxiety or false evidence appearing real (F.E.A.R.).

To stay in peace, you must discern when the enemy spirit is coming against you so you can recognize him immediately and then bind and rebuke him away, causing him to flee. If you let thoughts ruminate for more than a minute, the enemy has got you. Let's say you are driving down the road, and someone cuts you off or makes you slow down. What would you do? If I was driving, I would say nothing and treat them like Christ would want me to and that is with love, stay at peace, and maybe even speak out a loving prayer such as "Lord, I command the enemy to be gone from that person and I declare that the presence of the Lord envelop them in their car in Jesus' name!" I have prayed that prayer many, many times. Unfortunately, some people (even those who attend church regularly), would get upset and spew out negative words from their mouth at them, possibly honk their horns to try to make them move over, or even wait to see an opportunity to cut them off to get them back. Crazy enemy behavior! Is that what Jesus would want us to do? I think not. Therefore, a person who gets irritated would have a spirit of frustration or anger and take an offense against them, and that would cause them to react with anger to the driver of the other car thinking, "you can't slow me down or make me do what you want." So, if you sense that you are getting ready to lose your cool in that situation, you need to speak out loud, "I bind you spirit of anger in the name of Jesus, go!" and then you will get your peace back and it will not affect you negatively. Try it next time.

My mentor made me aware that if I ever was not at peace or felt uncomfortable, that it was always the enemy that was trying to steal my peace. At first, I did not comprehend what he meant because I had not felt at peace for about sixteen years due to others in my family or a spouse who was always striving. He told me that eventually I would get my peace back that I'd been waiting so long for and then be able to teach and train others in the world how to stay at peace every day. I am now experiencing the peace that he talked about and this book is one of the ways the Lord is going to help others learn to walk in peace every day of their life. It is a most beautiful life living in peace all the time, loving on other people that don't know peace, and helping them change their old mindsets from the enemy to Jesus.

Below are some additional examples how the enemy can steal your peace, as all have spirits that are ultimately behind each of them:

- Fear of the unknown (financially, health related, relationally with your spouse, children, or friends, etc.)
- Anger at someone who wronged you or over a situation that harmed you either emotionally, physically or financially – taking an offense
- Depressed over something bad that happened to you or someone you loved in the past that hurt you
- Rejection from people or a family member
- Selfish fleshly desires
- Hopeless that your situation in life will never improve
- Prideful about yourself and your position in life, job, or ministry
- Envious of another person or situation
- Greedy for accumulating wealth for personal gain
- Sexually desiring to please yourself in an ungodly way

So, whenever you are able to identify that you feel fearful, anxious, angry, depressed, rejected, or hopeless - you know that the enemy is on you trying to hurt you and you need to take your authority in Christ and speak out loud to command the spirits to go from you. Living in peace every day should be normal and if you are not experiencing it, then you have an enemy problem that is either affecting you or someone else who is in your presence.

So what should you do if you have to live with someone that causes you to lose your peace and you cannot get away from them? Often times, you may be married to someone that strives all the time and is anxious, fearful, or controlling, and it causes you to lose your peace when you're around them. In those cases, you need to try to minimize your time around them until they are able to see for themselves that they are being affected by enemy spirits and have them commanded out. If you have a child that is a teenager and is always causing havoc, until they get set free - you may need to limit your time around them even though it may be challenging since they live with you. You can still stay calm and keep your cool and not allow yourself to lose your peace. If they verbally go off on you, then you may need to walk into a different room or walk outside, but try to limit your verbal comeback to them. This can be extremely difficult under the heat of the moment and since you have responded in kind for many months or years, your mindset needs to be changed and takes great restraint of what your flesh would like to do.

The intention of this chapter is to help you recognize that if you are not at peace, it is an enemy issue and not a physical or circumstantial one like it may appear to be. Just think back to how many times that you have not been at peace in your life or the most significant instances that you can think of.

Perhaps one day you were informed, like I was one time, that you no longer would have a job. In my case, the Lord told me an hour ahead of time that my boss was going to call me and let me know that I would no longer be needed as the company had sold off a division of their business. I had never lost a job in my life before this (about

27 straight years) and could have suffered tremendous anxiety about what the future held. Instead of getting into fear, I was actually excited because in my spirit - I had wanted to do ministry full time and I knew this was part of the process of me transitioning out of the financial services technology industry and into ministry. I was so excited because I knew that was what was in my heart, so I became very happy and joyful of this news. I was at complete peace and excited while my wife started to get hit with fear and worry about finances in the future and how we would pay our bills, food, rent, and mortgage on our home that her son and his wife were renting from us at a reduced rental amount, etc. My current situation was that I had taken on debt of $50,000 over four years by helping my stepsons as they could not pay for some of their bills for college loans, car repairs, other purchases, needing a 50% discount on their rent, etc. I took on most of their utilities and one year allowed my stepson not to pay any rent because he lost his job. The Lord had me take on many of their debts for them to show them what a godly man would do for them in an extreme act of sacrificial love to dramatically impact them at a deep level.

The morning after I was told that I was going to be without a job in two months (they gave me two months' notice), I went for a run and asked the Lord what I should do next for employment or income. He told me clearly not to do a thing but that He would bring the next job to me. A few hours later my manager who had told me the day before that I was no longer going to have a job, called to tell me that the company that acquired a portion of our company's business needed someone with my expertise and that I should talk to them about a job. I talked to them and they said that although they could not offer me a full time employee position, they would love for me to be an independent contractor to help them write up contracts between their company and all the core processing companies that managed the financial data for banks and credit unions in the United States. The Lord blessed me and increased my annual income from $150k at my previous job to $170k. What a deal! Then two months later when I no longer worked for my previous company, I received a one-time severance check for $50,000 which was exactly the amount of debt that I had accrued due to paying for my stepsons' bills for four years and all of a sudden, I was debt free. God is so good when we do not get into fear and strife and stay in His peace so He can provide for our needs.

You can see by not getting into fear and trusting the Lord the day that I learned I was going to lose my job, it allowed me to stay in my peace and be blessed. Therefore, I want to impress on everyone that we need to shift our thinking and mindsets from earthly enemy fear to heavenly godly peace and live that way the rest of our lives. The enemy is real and wants to cause you to live in fear, worry, anger, etc. every day and that is NOT what a Christian is called to operate out of. We are to live every day of our life in peace. If you are not able to live in peace, then it is always the enemy affecting you every time.

Isaiah 26:3-4 NKJV, "[3] You will keep him in perfect peace, Whose mind is stayed on You, Because he trusts in You. [4] Trust in the Lord forever, For in YAH, the LORD, is everlasting strength."

CHAPTER 3

We are Not of this World

John 16:33 NKJV "These things I have spoken to you, that in Me you may have peace. In the world you will have tribulation; but be of good cheer, I have overcome the world." When we give our lives to Christ, we can officially tap into all the power and authority that Christ had because He was not of this world and therefore neither are we as our spirits are now from heavenly places. We should also be living our lives in the same peace that He walked in every day. Jesus said in John 14:12 NKJV "Most assuredly, I say to you, he who believes in Me, the works that I do he will do also; and greater works than thee he will do, because I go to My Father." Because we are not of this world, just like our Heavenly Father, we should behave entirely different than the world does.

We should be living the victorious Christian life versus those living as non-believers in the world. Christians are all living in different stages of our walks. Recognize that those of the world who are not believers in Christ will behave in ways that are not Christ-like. People should see a tremendous difference between those who are living Christian lives vs. those who aren't, but many are walking at various levels depending on their maturity in Christ. Those who are brand new believers will still have remnants of their previous life to get freed from which include mindsets that were carnal and not spiritual. Those who are more mature should be walking every day in the full authority of Christ and when they pray for people, they should expect to see many get healed instantly. They should hear from the Lord and give words of knowledge and prophecy to people, and they most certainly should be walking in peace and love every day of their life.

So why don't we see more Christians walking out a life of power, love, and peace every day? There's a myriad of reasons such as they have not been taught correctly, the enemy has stolen from them the proper understanding of the scriptures, they have enemy spirits that have afflicted them since receiving mother and/or father wounds as a child that they have never been delivered from, etc. A person who receives the Holy Spirit is a major benefactor to being able to walk more in the full power of the Lord. Praying in tongues is like receiving an AK-47 gun compared to fighting the enemy with your bare hands as a basic Christian. It supercharges you to being able to hear from the Lord more clearly as well as discerning spirits that are affecting you and other people. It baffles me how a pastor cannot tell everyone in his congregation that they need to ask the Lord for the gift of tongues in order to be a more effective Christian for the Lord against the enemy. We also should see a genuine change inside of us that takes us out of the world, per se, and allows us to walk around as if Christ was actually inside of us (which He is supposed to be!). When we walk around in everyday life, we should be loving and have peace all around us wherever we go. We should have people that look forward to seeing us every day instead of wanting to run away from us.

Have you ever been around a person at church that only complains about others or their own situation every time you see them? How does that make you feel? It makes me feel sad, depressed, and sometimes sick in my spirit because what is on them gets on me. Who wants to be slimed every time you talk to that person and what ends up happening is you try to avoid them in the future. Come on, I know you have done this before as I have and everyone else has if they are honest! No one wants to be around someone that is a Debbie Downer because it literally brings you down and sucks the life right out of you. If you're the type of person that constantly has negative things happening all around you and you choose to spew your negativity onto others, have you ever lost friends or seen new acquaintances avoid you and walk the other way when they see you at church? It is because that is what the world is all about and they do not know any better. We are not of this world like He was not of this world and therefore, we should speak positively and in love and always be at peace which will attract others to us instead of repelling them to run the opposite direction. By speaking into your circumstances, you allow the enemy to control your thoughts even more and then you never see your life circumstances change to the positive.

John 17: 11-23 NKJV Jesus states "[11] Now I am no longer in the world, but these are in the world, and I come to You. Holy Father, keep through Your name those whom You have given Me, that they may be one as We are. [12] While I was with them in the world, I kept them in Your name. Those whom You gave Me I have kept; and none of them is lost except the son of perdition, that the Scripture might be fulfilled. [13] But now I come to You, and these things I speak in the world, that they may have My joy fulfilled in themselves. [14] I have given them Your word; and the world has hated them because they are not of the world, just as I am not of the world. [15] I do not pray that You should take them out of the world, but that You should keep them from the evil one. [16] They are not of the world, just as I am not of the world. [17] Sanctify them by Your truth. Your word is truth. [18] As You sent Me into the world, I also have sent them into the world. [19] And for their sakes I sanctify Myself, that they also may be sanctified by the truth. [20] I do not pray for these alone, but also for those who will believe in Me through their word; [21] that they all may be one, as You, Father, are in Me, and I in You; that they also may be one in Us, that the world may believe that You sent Me. [22] And the glory which You gave Me I have given them, that they may be one just as We are one: [23] I in them, and You in Me; that they may be made perfect in one, and that the world may know that You have sent Me, and have loved them as You have loved Me."

Therefore, since Christ was not of this world and we have Christ living in our spirits, then we should be walking around like Christ every day. Do you think Christ was ever not at peace? Even when the Pharisees came to question Him with hate and contempt in their hearts, He still had peace as He corrected them which irritated them even more because they could not get him to lose his peace. Even when the crowds tried to gather around Him, He was able to translate away to safety and avoid any real confrontations until He was ready to give Himself up. How would you like to be able to stay in a position of peace no matter who came up to engage you in a battle of words to try to cause you to get upset? You can do it but it will take a little practice and help from the Holy Spirit to keep your peace.

When we approach life from the vantage point that we are really not from this world but from above, then we are able to love others that are hard to love in extreme ways by not ever striving with them because we can see ourselves loving them as Christ's ambassadors. We are on earth to be Christ's representatives and on assignment to bring love, joy, and peace to everyone we engage with. Therefore, if someone tries to come after you with a verbal barrage of hatred, it should not faze you one iota. It is not pleasant to have to endure but you should be able to bite your tongue and take it because your spirit can sense that the person who is chewing you out is not a believer or if he professes to be then is not in the right space spiritually. You should give a person more grace when you realize that they are not as strong in the Lord as you are, and you can turn the other cheek and smile at them in love. I know of a father to a woman who truly believes that he is a great Christian. Yet everyone that works for him, when asked how amazing is he to work for, gives you a look like "Are you kidding me – he is horrible!" He berates people verbally and if they do not do exactly what he wants, he'll go off on them until they feel like an ant ready to be stepped on. He visits prisoners and gives money away yet treats his own children with contempt and even will disown them if they do not do exactly what he commands. It is sad because this man never knew what it was like to be loved by a father so is behaving out of his own pain and understanding and gets hit with the enemy frequently telling him that all people have to do exactly what he says or else he will take things into his own hands and try to force them. No love and no peace for anyone in his family with very few friends and children who have hurt everyone that they came into relationship with. Out of all that pain, they are all suffering from physical pains and diseases in their bodies.

My mindset started to change when I began to understand who I really was in Christ. My purpose on earth was to do what the Lord wanted me to do. He wanted me to love on a hurting world of people and teach them how to be free from enemy torment and live in more peace. I would need to exhibit greater patience and tolerance for people that were not behaving like they should instead of taking an offense and causing strife or arguing. If a stepchild does something that is obviously not correct, instead of speaking a strong word of correction that they could not handle, you may need to avoid the conversation altogether in order to keep the peace and then let the Lord come in and do the correcting via consequences from Him. Therefore, you would keep the relationship with the child instead of losing it forever and ultimately allow the Lord's correction to take place perfectly instead of taking it into your own hands.

When you start to understand that those who are true Christians are actually called to sacrifice their own lives for others in order to bring about the hurting people coming to the Lord, then you are able to endure the enemy's words coming through those people without responding in kind. So think twice or three times before speaking to someone who is obviously being tormented by the enemy and realize that it is not worth it to try to engage with them during the heat of the moment and the wisest choice is to avoid them altogether. We are truly not from this world as our spirits are from the Lord so ultimately - we are just here to help others that are not as far along as we are in our Christian walk.

Chapter 4

Don't Look Upon Your Circumstances

Everyone experiences people in their lives that affect them and various challenges that happen to them. This is called their circumstances. It is what is real and tangible and is the here and now situation of events that you call your life. If you are currently working a dead-end job that barely pays the bills each month, then that is your current situation. If your son or daughter was molested and is now a terror to live around and makes your life miserable – then you are not currently enjoying a peace filled life and your circumstances are not easy. If your spouse was rejected and controlled by her father and unloved by her mother and now treats you with extreme control, manipulation, deceit, sexual perversion, and makes your life a living hell behind closed doors, that is circumstantially what your life currently is but is that what your life will be like in the future?

So many people look at their current situation in life as what it will always be. If they are miserable and feel depressed because the past thirty years have been nothing but hell on earth, they expect the rest of their life will continue to be horrible and they have nothing to look forward to because it will never change. They are correct if they do not change their mindsets and what words come out of their mouths as they will most likely not see change. They do not have the faith to believe that the Lord will change their circumstances to become far better than they can imagine. In most cases, it just takes a shift of their mindsets from the enemy's territory to heavenly and godly thinking where anything is possible and that God wants to bless them greatly and improve their circumstances. They may have been told this several times before but they never got the revelation into their spirits to cause them to really believe that it is possible and then to speak it out of their mouth daily.

In Romans 4:17 NKJV - Abraham was praised for his faith stating (as it is written, "I have made you a father of many nations") in the presence of Him whom he believed – God, who gives life to the dead and calls those things which do not exist as though they did;" Therefore he did not look upon his current circumstances as though they would always be that way (although with his situation of his future descendants, he did have a weak moment of faith and tried to take his destiny into his own hands by making children through his wife's servant Hagar which produced Ishmael). Abraham and his nephew Lot came to need more land because they were being blessed so much that the current property they inhabited was not able to contain both of them. He allowed Lot to choose where to go live but unfortunately, Lot looked upon his circumstances and chose to live in the more productive looking land of Sodom and Gomorrah which later was destroyed by God due to the rampant sexual sins that were prevalent along with the practice of homosexuality. Abraham was left to live in a much more desolate place. Instead of being sad, depressed, and speaking out loud "Why did I allow my nephew Lot to choose the financially blessed city of Sodom and Gomorrah and now I'm stuck

56

living in a hot desert that nothing good can come from." He decided that the Lord would bless his hands wherever he went so called things that were not as though they were and was blessed even greater.

Noah was told by God to start building a huge boat even though it had never rained on earth before. God warned him that He was going to flood the earth because man had become so evil and then He would start over with Noah's family to populate the earth. Noah began to build the largest boat ever and it took him almost 100 years to complete it. Can you imagine how much ridicule he received from all the people that were his neighbors and former friends? He had to have strong faith that he'd heard the Lord correctly to spend so much of his life on this project when it had never rained on earth before, so no one had a clue what a flood would be like. Imagine if the Lord told you that your circumstances would dramatically change but you had to wait 100 years to see it come to pass! How many of you could do what the Lord told you to do instead of listening to your family and friends tell you that you were crazy? Most might try it for a week or possibly a month, and maybe a few would even wait for a year or a little longer, but to wait most of your lifetime to see it come to pass – now that is great faith and determination not to look upon circumstances. When the raindrops finally started to fall – Noah's circumstances changed from a place of ridicule to a place of refuge and tremendous appreciation from his family and the animals that he took in.

Here's what I'm trying to convey. Life and death are in the power of our tongues, so we must never speak into our circumstances as they appear today through complaining or saying they'll never change because we give the enemy strength to keep us under those circumstances. If we continue to only speak out what we are currently seeing with our own eyes with no faith to see it change, we'll continue to receive what we speak. If we have no peace in our current situation and speak out that our life is over and nothing will ever change – then our lives will look the same and probably not change, and we'll usually become more depressed as the enemy grows in strength to control our minds.

You have to change your old mindsets and speak words of life to be able to change your current circumstances. You must never speak out loud how horrible your life is and that you will never enjoy a good life. Yes, your current life's circumstances may very well be awful, but you will never have peace if you keep speaking out how miserable your life is over and over. You must change your words before you will see your circumstances change for the positive. In other words – instead of saying "My life is awful and will never change" you need to be speaking "Thank you Jesus that my life is changing and I have peace, love, and joy every day!"

I remember when my daughter wanted to live with me full time instead of half of the time (every other week) after my first wife divorced me. Her mother would not allow her to live with me full time even though we came to an agreement in our divorce settlement (thru mediation), that our children could self-determine if they wanted to live more with one parent than the other. My youngest son had determined he wanted to live more with his mother so I did not fight it even though I loved him and missed seeing him as often as I would have liked. One day my daughter received some harsh words from her mother in front of her girlfriend which hurt her. She decided that she wanted to come live with me full time, so I allowed her to because of our self-determination clause in our agreement. Her mother could not stand that our daughter defied her control and came to live with me full time so took me to court to try to force our daughter to live with her half of the time. She did not represent the whole truth of the situation when we went to court and was represented by an attorney while I had none because I was handed the court appearance on a Friday at 5 pm and the court date was the following Monday morning which left no time to arrange for my attorney to accompany me. The Lord told me that He would be my attorney and not to worry. The judge was harsh to me and said I had to make my daughter see her mother every other week or else I would go to jail. This made my daughter very sad because she loved me as we were very close and wanted to live in peace with me.

So what did I do? I could have listened to the enemy and lost my peace and become depressed because I could not make my daughter live with me full time since the judge issued his warning and I did not believe in taking ANYONE to court because that is not how the Lord wants His people to proceed. He wants to be our protector and cause circumstances to change supernaturally based on our faith. My daughter pleaded with her mother several times over the next few months to allow her to live with me full time but to no avail and was resigned to going back and forth every other week until she turned 18.

Instead of looking at the circumstances and giving up and losing my peace every day, I chose to praise the Lord every morning for at least thirty minutes that I had full custody of her and she would live with me in peace. Every day I thanked God for giving my daughter to me full time. Every day my daughter lived with her mom, she complained that her mom would never let her go which was particularly frustrating for her because her mom allowed her brother to live with her full time and I did not take her to court to make him live with me half of the time. So this seemed somewhat analogous to the Hebrew people and the Pharaoh of Egypt where Moses kept telling him to "Let my people go!" and Pharaoh hardened his heart and said no. I told my daughter to keep her faith positive and stay in peace because the Lord would come through for us. Month after month I continued to thank the Lord that I had full custody of my daughter and then after six months of thanking the Lord, one evening I received a call from my daughter that her mother no longer wanted her and to consider her new step mom as her mom. So she dropped her off and I now had my daughter full time! She was so happy and thankful that I did not give up and continued to battle in the spirit to see it come to pass for her. I could have gotten down and given up a month into the circumstances not changing and then lost my peace and became totally despondent but the Lord rewarded me for staying positive and speaking out what I wanted to see manifest in the physical. You have to fight in the spirit to see your circumstances change and not give up after just a few weeks or months of declaring and thanking the Lord for victory and not seeing your situation change in the physical.

Another situation was when I had continued to take on more debt for my stepsons year after year and went from owing no money prior to my 2nd marriage in 2009 to accumulating $50,000 in credit card debt by 2012. I could have looked at my circumstances as hopeless and spoke out that I would never be able to pay off the debt and then declare bankruptcy and then lost all my peace and moved into a state of fear and worry. Instead, I kept declaring that my debts were paid off and stayed positive month after month, year after year. It was extremely hard because I kept taking on more debt for my wife's sons as the Lord told me I had to love them like Christ which was way more extreme than I ever would have imagined. I kept loving them and taking on more and more debt every year. Eventually I got a call from my manager at Intuit Financial Services who let me know that I was being let go due to part of our company being sold off.

I really could have listened to the enemy whispering to me that my life was over now but instead I stayed close to the Lord and the next day learned that I had an opportunity to work for the company that purchased a division of ours and two months later made a clean transition from one job to the next as my last day at Intuit was on a Friday and my first day with the new company was the following Monday. My severance check which was supposed to help me live to find a new job was for the exact amount of the debt I took on for my stepsons the previous 4 years. I was so excited to deposit my $50,000 check and because I'd had lent my SUV to my stepson for 9 months, did not have it to drive my check to the bank to deposit it so had to ride my bike from Cicero, IN to Noblesville, IN which was about 10 miles one way to my bank, but if felt so good to finally be able to pay off all my debt and then make even more money with my new company.

I kept my peace and did not look upon my circumstances throughout the whole four years and complain every day (although I must admit there were times the enemy hit me). I learned so much from that circumstance and now can share as an example to encourage you. If God did it for me then he will do it for you as long as you stay positive and in peace. You can do it!

When my daughter was a senior at Hamilton Heights High School in Arcadia, IN she applied for a couple of colleges and was accepted at a few. She decided to start attending IUPUI (Indiana University – Purdue University – at Indianapolis). I had no money to pay for her college. Even though I made $170,000 a year at that time, I had no money available for my daughter because I had to keep helping my stepsons in significant ways and had been paying some child support even though I had shared custody due to having a higher income than my ex-wife.

I could have looked upon my circumstances and became sad and depressed that I could not afford to pay for her college but instead, I thanked God that I would have the money to cover her and she would have no issues. We applied for a 21st Century Indiana Scholarship which was usually only given to those that did not make that much money. Even though I made a lot of money, I had none left due to taking on my stepsons' debts, paying child support, tithing 20% of my gross income per the Lord (part of sowing into the Kingdom and out of it received His double blessing anointing). So again, I thanked God that my daughter was going to be approved for the scholarship every day. A few months later – we received news that she was indeed approved! Faith and trust can move mountains and usually do when we do not give up and keep our peace and faith on. Doubt and speaking words of death will produce sadness and badness.

One day I had been unceremoniously asked to leave a church that I'd prayed for people to be healed at in Fishers, IN. They offered what were called Healing Rooms. I did nothing wrong but the pastor at the church had believed someone close to me who lied about me instead of believing my truth of the matter in the situation. I could have lost my peace and become very angry and furious for this because it was totally wrong and a complete injustice in every way imaginable – but I chose not to strive. Instead, I stayed positive and within months - the Lord rewarded me to be the Director of my own Healing Rooms. The church that I left went from offering their healing services twice a month for 2 hours a day to just once a month for 3 hours. The Lord asked me how often I wanted to be open and for how long. I told Him I really wanted to offer it every Saturday and to be open a minimum of 4 hours. He told me that He would honor me and that it would be blessed and rapidly grow to one of the busiest Healing Rooms in the Midwest. I was concerned that I would not have enough people to come alongside of me but He said that He would provide. I also told Him that I would like to allow the Holy Spirit to completely flow and not have to limit someone to fifteen minutes like the other Healing Rooms I had served under. He told me that is exactly what He wanted me to do as well. Yay God!

We had many people coming in from all corners of the state of Indiana that not only dealt with praying for physical pains but also got to many of their root issues which was because of demonic spirits that were tormenting them through various access points (generational sins and curses, mother and/or father wounds that developed into a Jezebel controlling and manipulative spirit, the Leviathan spirit of pride and twisting of truth which often gave people back and neck pain that would never be healed through regular general prayer). We soon became the busiest Healing Rooms in the state of Indiana as more people came to us from around the state and even as far away as Kentucky, Ohio, Illinois, Michigan, North Carolina, and Canada! Had I looked upon my circumstances, I could have given up on my ever working in Healing Rooms again and decided that the enemy was stronger than me, but that was not who I was and I would never be defeated by him. I was a mighty man of God and would not be stopped by a Jezebel spirit – my goal was to deliver more people from Jezebel than anyone as I had an extreme anointing for helping people get freed from the hardest spirit on earth to be set free from. Yay God again!

One man had given everything he had to love on a woman that had been rejected by many men throughout her life yet he was determined that he would help her get healed and restored and that together they would help thousands upon thousands in ministries. Unfortunately, the enemy was very strong on her and told him he had to stop doing ministry and focus on his marriage to her while she was going to still do ministry. The Lord told him he needed to separate from her and that in doing so, He would bless his ministry greatly and that He would finish what the man had started in getting his wife set free and then bring her back to him and join in the rapidly growing ministry. The enemy was very strong on her and she actually came against him and lied to many of their mutual friends as well as the pastors at their church.

Unfortunately, the senior pastor at their church refused to talk to him and help hold his wife accountable for the horrible abuse she did to him for many years. The senior pastor actually told him to leave his church and never talk to any of his congregation again. The Lord showed the man a dream a few months later that He had his back and that He would deal with the pastor for encouraging his wife to actually divorce him instead of holding her accountable and getting her delivered to save her from her fourth divorce. It was the ultimate slap in his face for all that he did for her and her children but he chose not to strive and eventually, the Lord redeemed what he had gone through and blessed him greatly in ministry while dealing firmly with the senior pastor. His former wife was also corrected by the Lord to bring her to come to the end of her sin.

A person may think that they can get away with sinning and that other people will not find out but the Lord will expose it for what it is and unless the person repents, they will have major consequences in life. The Lord does not take lightly when a person abuses an innocent person and lies about them and then has accomplices that join in. He will expose all sin and reveal the truth to the world if He has to in order to bring about true repentance and restoration. So keep your peace on and realize that the Lord has got your back and will reveal the truth in its due season and make right what the enemy meant for evil.

One time I was working for a company that processed products that were either recalled due to defects or destroyed if needed. I was making just enough money to pay my bills and began to grow tired of working for them after almost six months, wanting the Lord to change my circumstances. I did not complain but rather asked Him to change them. The Lord spoke to me at the beginning of that next week and told me that something was going to change for me by the end of the week that would make me happy and be a good thing.

I waited and continued to look forward to the end of the week. On Friday I had left work at the end of the day and started to walk towards my car in the parking lot thinking to myself "Wonder what God was talking about because now the week is over and I am still working at this place that I do not want to work at anymore." As I was walking out to the parking lot my manager was walking towards me and said she wanted to talk to me. I knew in my spirit that she was going to tell me that my services were no longer needed, and I was so excited because I did not want to work there anymore (I know – sounds crazy but hey – when you are tired of working at a place, it is time to move on). Sure enough, she got very solemn and said she was very sad to have to inform me that I was no longer needed. My reaction was one of excitement and thankfulness and I even told her "When God closes a door, He opens a window of new opportunity" and I thanked her graciously for letting me know. She was shocked! She said that she had never had anyone that responded that way to news of unemployment in her entire career.

She did not know that I was not like most employees. I had no job, had lots of bills to pay, and I was totally excited (Woo-Hoo God)! I had to give plasma again in order to make my payments the next week, but I was totally at peace and grateful to be able to meet some folks that I would have never gotten to know. I thought, how funny Lord, I used to make $170,000 a year and now here I am giving my own blood in order to make $75 a week to pay my bills and eat.

The Lord had told me a few weeks prior to write a book about deliverance from a controlling and manipulative spirit named Jezebel that had wreaked havoc in people's marriages and in the church and ministries. He told me that the book would change people's lives and save thousands and thousands of marriages all over the world. I could not get the book done as fast as I wanted because I was working at the recall company. Once I no longer had the job, I was able to finally get the book complete in a matter of weeks and then when it came out people that read it started to get delivered from Jezebel and Leviathan spirits (the book was called *Restored to Freedom*) and I saw lives changed and so many marriages were saved from divorce. As you can see, I was able to keep my peace on and not lose it to fear - all by not looking upon my circumstances and speaking out words of negativity that were opposite of what I wanted to see. Eventually the Lord blessed my book and told me to write a second one while I was waiting for a few people to endorse my first. I said to the Lord "What! No one writes two books at one time" and he responded with "You are not 'no one' – and you have a double portion anointing on your life!" I was so excited to hear that and told Him thanks. He said because of what I willingly had done for Him and for enduring such an extreme tribulation, He would reward me for my faithfulness in suffering for the Kingdom. I started writing my second book and it was complete within about seventeen days. It was called *Jesus Loves to Heal Through You* and has shown hundreds and hundreds of people how to pray more effectively and start seeing miracles when they pray.

After I had written my first two books, the Lord brought me another temporary full-time job of scoring tests for high school and middle school children. It did not pay me enough to cover my monthly bills but the Lord told me that I would start seeing more donations come into my ministry. More books would sell and change the lives of more people as I would start speaking in more churches that would take free will offerings for me. I took the job while not speaking into my circumstances that I would not have enough money to cover my bills. I kept my peace on and did not get into fear or worry. Sure enough, people started randomly donating into my ministry at my Healing Rooms, at the churches I attended, online on my website, and I started seeing more of my books sell and I started speaking in churches. I could see that the Lord was growing my ministry and was blessing me for staying in peace and trusting that He would provide for all my needs. Other people could also see the Lord's blessings and favor and many that thought wrongly about me were finally seeing that I was really a godly man and there was nothing that I would not do to help other people to get freedom from the enemy. The Lord had my back and there was nothing He would not do for me as long as I stayed humble and pure before Him and kept my peace and love on.

I ended up finishing my work at the test scoring company and had no work to do as the Lord told me that He was now transitioning me into full time ministry. While I had no job, He told me to write my next two books which were *Loving Like Christ: How to Love the Hard to Love People in Your Life* and then *Waking the Lion Within: Reclaiming Your Position in Christ* which is about helping men that were operating under the Ahab spirit to become vibrant, mighty men of valor spiritually. I wrote the first book in three weeks and the second book in three more weeks. The Lord then started to promote me through various TV shows (The Harvest Show on LeSEA Broadcasting – the former Lester Sumrall show that I watched as a teenager, TBN in Indianapolis, Atlanta Live, Club 36 in North Augusta, and SC and WGGS in Greenville, SC). I was then asked to come to Dallas to be interviewed on a rapidly growing TV/Internet live streaming station called Meet the Messenger and there were other churches and TV stations around the country that wanted me to come and speak/minister. I also started having people contact me around the world (South Africa, the UK, Pakistan, India, Africa, etc.) to have me do Skype/Facebook video ministry sessions with them in order to get them delivered from tormenting spirits so they could function in peace. It was amazing to see the Lord open up so many doors to so many hurting people and have them set free from a lifetime of pain.

One night, I was ministering on Facebook video to a woman from India who was hurt deeply by her father and others in her life. While ministering to her, I received a Facebook message from a woman in Tokyo who wanted ministry and then a woman from the state of Washington who also wanted help. The Lord told me to get ready because my ministry was going to grow exponentially.

When you remain in peace and do not allow the enemy to have a right to keep you under his circumstances, there is no limit on what God is able to do for you and peace should be normal every day of your life. Yes, I realize if you are living with someone that the enemy is affecting in a strong way that it's hard to keep your peace on but realize that you do have total control over yourself and how you react and what you say out of your mouth. If your spouse divorced you after you loved them like Christ and He told you that they would come back to you and repent for what they did and then promote you for what you did for them, then stand in faith as long as it takes, walk in peace, and rejoice every day because it will come to pass.

Exodus 14:14 states "The Lord will fight for you, and you shall hold your peace." This means that if you stay in peace, He will rise up and take on the enemy on your behalf. I have seen this over and over again in my life. There is something so peaceful about realizing that we do not need to look upon our circumstances and get into fear because God has got our back. He will literally go to battle for you and defeat the enemy in your life whether it is a mean, vindictive spouse, conniving former friend, controlling and pride filled pastor, disrespectful child, even a court appearance where the judge unjustly accused you of something that was not true based on the lies of another person. The Lord wants to protect His people but you have to get in proper position to receive His taking on your battles. You cannot be sinning in private or in public and disregarding purity or having behavior that the Lord would not have you live in. That will block the ability for the Lord to protect you and give the enemy access to hurt you and cause you to lose your peace. As long as you're living a life that is aligned with the Word, there is nothing He will not do to help you and bless you.

The Lord expects you to behave in a calm and godly way, especially after you have read this book, because He wants his bride to be pure and blameless before Him and not to get into contentions and arguments with anyone at any time, ever. You should be unoffendable – never taking an offense against anyone that has said or done anything to hurt you. You need to forgive them and give them to the Lord. If they need corrected, the Lord will do the correcting and shaking in a mighty and perfect way.

He wants you to remain at peace every day for the rest of your life and not get into fear and worry about your finances, your relationships, your health, anything. He also wants you to help others that are in your sphere of influence to walk in the same peace that you walk in, and never get into fear, worry, anger, envy, greed, pride, etc. We must never look upon our circumstances and allow them to control us. We must stay in our peace and watch our circumstances come in line with our faith and trust that the Lord has got our back and we will see our declared destiny come to pass.

CHAPTER 5

Be Like Christ

We are called to love like Christ but what does that look like and who can actually do it? Jesus showed us many examples of how to love like He did in His everyday life. When he was a young man, he showed us by never getting into strife with anyone. He didn't pick on his younger siblings or disrespect his parents (although one time he forgot to tell his parents where he was going and showed up teaching older Jewish leaders in a synagogue). He was gentle of spirit and had complete compassion for all that were hurting and in pain. Everywhere he walked, he wanted to help those less fortunate. He discerned what a person was feeling inside of their hearts without having to ask them what they were feeling. He knew that the woman at the well had gone from husband to husband to husband searching for true love and was able to explain to her that what she really was looking for was right in front of her. She needed peace and to rest in the Lord's peace.

To be like Christ means that we walk in His same power and authority but also to love everyone no matter what they do to us. We need to never get into strife with anyone, ever. Ponder this, someone that thinks they know about a particular situation or interpreting a scripture, but you realize they are completely off the mark. Should you point out to them that they have no idea what they are talking about and ridicule them for their ignorance on the matter? Should you explain piously that you know more than they do about the situation or scripture and that they have no idea what they are talking about? What do you think will ensue should you take that stance? Most likely, they will feel offended and then speak words of strife back to you causing you to lose your peace and they will become angry with you. Therefore, the best stance would have been to let them think they are right and let it go to avoid strife. Sometimes wisdom dictates that we say nothing. Proverbs 17:14 NKJV "The beginning of strife is like releasing water; Therefore, stop contention before a quarrel starts."

I was in relationship with some people who thought they knew it all but unfortunately, much of the time they had no clue. I would sometimes offer what I knew to be the truth so that they would avoid making what could have been a significant mistake costing them their pride, money, and consequences. But often times, I had to choose to keep my mouth shut and avoid strife to then allow the Lord to correct them. Proverbs 3:12 NKJV "For whom the Lord loves He corrects, Just as a father the son in whom he delights." It was very hard at times because I knew what the pending outcome was going to be, but they would not receive my insight so had to let them learn the hard way.

Can you imagine what Jesus had to endure? He walked around every day with his disciples who were clueless and yet He chose not to get into strife with them telling them "Hey guys, you are fools and have no idea what you are talking about, so listen to Me, the Son of God, and keep your mouths quiet! Oh – and take really good notes because soon I will not be here anymore and you better not forget what

I am teaching you!" There were many times that He had to bite his tongue and not speak out words that could hurt them because He knew what they were thinking. Instead, He showed godly love, compassion, and restraint realizing that they were just ignorant of the truth of various matters and realities. I imagine that He probably just laughed to Himself in love quite a bit and chose not to mock them proudly as His flesh could have done. Peter assuredly said and did many things that caused Jesus to just shake his head and think "Wow – is he ever going to get it?" Good thing Jesus learned to keep His good sense of humor from his Father.

Jesus never made fun of someone or acted like he was 'all that' because that was not who He was. He knew that the people that came to Him to learn were often times seeking peace in their own lives. He could sense and know that just like today – people were searching for a real inner peace in their lives who were tormented in fear, doubt, anger, and worse.

Think about Zacchaeus. His name in Hebrew means "pure" and "innocent" which would appear very ironic due to the type of work that he did. He was a descendant of Abraham and was an example of Jesus' personal, earthly mission to bring salvation to the lost. He was also a tax collector which meant he was despised like a traitor because he was working for the Roman Empire and not helping out his Jewish brotherhood. His position would have carried both importance and wealth and therefore he was a person that probably had few friends and many enemies. He was most likely familiar with receiving looks of disgust and anger by many who saw him walking the streets of his day. You can imagine that many people who walked around him probably whispered and even spoke out loud negative words to him because they despised him for taking their money and keeping some for himself. Many probably even hated him and wished he was not alive. Jesus knew who he really was more than Zacchaeus knew himself and so wanted to connect him to his destiny by calling it out in him.

The story of Zacchaeus has been used by some to exemplify the saying of Jesus: "Blessed are the pure of heart, for they shall see God" (in Matthew 5:8), because his name means 'pure.' Zacchaeus also becomes a contrast of character with the Rich Young Ruler in Luke 18:18-23. Both Zacchaeus and the Rich Young Ruler were wealthy men, but one was self-righteous and would not give up his money or possessions, while the other gave half of his possessions to feed the poor.

Luke 19:1-10 NKJV "[1] Then Jesus entered and passed through Jericho. [2] Now behold, there was a man named Zacchaeus who was a chief tax collector, and he was rich. [3] And he sought to see who Jesus was, but could not because of the crowd, for he was of short stature. [4] So he ran ahead and climbed up into a sycamore tree to see Him, for He was going to pass that way. [5] And when Jesus came to the place, He looked up and saw him, and said to him, "Zacchaeus, make haste and come down, for today I must stay at your house." [6] So he made haste and came down, and received Him joyfully. [7] But when they saw it, they all complained, saying, "He has gone to be a guest with a man who is a sinner!" [8] Then Zacchaeus stood and said to the Lord, "Look, Lord, I give half of my goods to the poor; and if I have taken anything from anyone by false accusation, I restore fourfold." [9] And Jesus said to him, "Today salvation has come to this house, because he also is a son of Abraham; [10] for the Son of Man has come to seek and to save that which was lost."

As you can imagine, if people of today saw a man of God coming to speak at their church and ended up going to a house of a man that caused the people of their community to be very poor while he was rich because of it (perhaps he owned several apartment complexes whose people could barely afford to live there) – what would their reaction be? They would speak out words of strife and not stay in peace out of their anger and resentment. Jesus knew who the man really was in Christ and that he ultimately had compassion on the people that he took taxes from. Jesus could have spoken words of condemnation and those around him would have cheered him on.

Instead, he stayed in peace and entered into relationship with Zacchaeus against the will of the people. How many times have you been put in a position where other people wanted you to be angry with someone and then you joined in to take on their offense against that person instead of discerning who they really were in Christ? Then later, you found out that what they were upset about was a total lie that you had believed for several years. The enemy is very sly to cause us to listen to him and his lies and not know the real truth in order to create dissension and strife.

It is so critical that we all listen to the Holy Spirit when assessing a person or situation and not jump to conclusions or join in the raucous crowd sentiments against someone or listen to gossip which contains half-truths or twisted lies. We must discern the truth and always stay in complete control of our emotions which can be very challenging if you have family members that are not close to the Lord and try to control and manipulate you to do things they want. The enemy will speak to them to try to force you to do what the enemy wants, and it is not fun standing up for what you know to be true and righteous while your family and former friends are verbally berating you, yelling and screaming, or posting messages on Facebook and other social media against you. So many innocent victims have been crucified before the world on Facebook and some never recover because their reputations have been forever tarnished and they were not strong enough to stand up to the spiritual attacks.

Jesus was our perfect example on how to keep from striving with other people and walking every day in peace. Just imagine how he was able to stay at peace every day when walking around with all those Pharisees and Jewish scribes that had envy and hatred in their hearts for Him.

How many days a month do you walk in total peace from the time you wake up until you lay down to sleep? In my life from age 31 through 47 - I had very few days of peace and most days were filled with extreme strife and chaos which was really exhausting. When you live with someone that constantly speaks out words that cause pain, hurt, and creates arguments - it makes it very challenging to keep your peace on to say the least. About the only thing that you can do in those situations is to try to stay away from those that create the strife as much as possible. Go for a walk if they will let you. Try to go for a drive to get away until you get your peace back which may be just an hour, several hours, or more.

Walking every day in peace like Christ involves looking at other people with empathy who strive and consider what their life must have been like when they grew up and avoid all words that could start strife. When you can see those who are hard to be around through the eyes of Christ, you can give more grace to them and allow them to speak words that would normally hurt you while keeping your peace and not retaliating in kind. The Lord gave you two ears and one mouth so while it is not fun to listen to words that cause you pain, you do have control over your responses with your tongue. If you cannot say something back in love then bite your tongue.

If you can develop your ability to discern in the Spirit deeper, you will know just by looking at someone how they grew up and what they have been through in their lives. Also, the Lord can speak to you and let you know what they have gone through. When you have a godly perspective to see the pain in someone, you will have a godly grace for their words of agony. Ask the Lord for greater discernment and to have your spiritual eyes opened to discern as Jesus did.

I used to have no discernment until after I attended a Morris Cerullo World Evangelism conference in 2009 and began to be mentored by a man who heard very clearly from the Lord which eventually allowed me to receive a much stronger gift of discernment than I ever had before. Anyone can hear the Lord's voice if they really want to and press in to know Him at a greater level. I highly advise that everyone ask the Lord for the gift of discernment because it is so desperately needed in order to know what a person can handle and what they cannot.

CHAPTER 6

Patience is a Virtue

When you decide that you will attempt to walk in peace every day for the rest of your life, you must learn how to show great patience with other people at a level that you may have never known before. I know for me personally, I was not much of a patient person until January of 2009 when the Lord changed me into seeing people through the eyes of Christ. I changed and became extremely patient in order to endure people that were extremely hard to be in their presence. Patience is a fruit of the Spirit and if you do not possess it, then you need to seek after it and learn to have it operate in your life every day. It is impossible to love anyone without being patient with them because people are not going to behave like you do and if you cannot be tolerant and show grace for them, you will speak out words that will generate strife. Once you have entered the world of strife, the enemy has a right to come in and cause all kinds of evil to hurt you and the person you are striving with and there is nothing that you can do to quicken the process of reversal. It just has to play its course and it may take hours, days, weeks, or months to heal.

I would like to now share several verses in the Bible that talk about the value of patience. Keep in mind how each verse relates to keeping one in peace, and they will go hand in hand. Each of the below verses are in the New King James Version:

1 Corinthians 13:4-5 "[4] Love suffers long and is kind; love does not envy; love does not parade itself, is not puffed up; [5] does not behave rudely, does not seek its own, is not provoked, thinks no evil;"

Suffering long means being patient. So, to truly love anyone you will have to be patient and you will have to often times suffer through it. Sometimes it's more suffering than what your mind will want to take but nonetheless, you will suffer and you will need to bite your tongue before speaking a word out to someone that will start an argument. Be quick to hear and slow to speak and think about it before you just blast someone with something hurtful out of your mouth.

Proverbs 14:29 "He who is slow to wrath has great understanding, But he who is impulsive exalts folly."

Being slow to wrath means being patient and not getting upset and speaking out words of harshness (that ultimately will start strife). It means that if you are slow to speak words out of your mouth that will hurt someone, you will have greater understanding (or wisdom). He who "speaks their mind" promotes folly or foolishness so be slow to speak and be wise.

Ephesians 4:1-3 "[1] I, therefore, the prisoner of the Lord, beseech you to walk worthy of the calling with which you were called, [2] with all lowliness and gentleness, with longsuffering, bearing with one another in love, [3] endeavoring to keep the unity of the Spirit in the bond of peace."

Paul talks about walking worthy with all humbleness, gentleness, and patience - enduring one another in love and keeping the unity of the Spirit in peace. What happens when you speak a harsh word to someone or retaliate in kind? You break the unity of the Spirit and there is no peace for hours, sometimes even days, weeks, or months. You simply cannot argue or contend with someone and retain peace at the same time. Sometimes you have to let the other person who thinks they know it all and think they are the perfect Christian speak out and behave like a fool while saying nothing to correct them for their own ignorance. It is called keeping the peace. Let the Lord do the correcting of them. He does a very good job and then we can stay at peace with them.

Romans 12:9-12 "[9] Let love be without hypocrisy. Abhor what is evil. Cling to what is good. [10] Be kindly affectionate to one another with brotherly love, in honor giving preference to one another; [11] not lagging in diligence, fervent in spirit, serving the Lord; [12] rejoicing in hope, patient in tribulation, continuing steadfastly in prayer;"

Loving someone without holding them to a higher standard than you would yourself can be challenging but needs to occur. Avoiding behaviors that are evil and drawing close to what is good is a must. Treating someone with kind affection and honoring them over yourself while serving the Lord and being hopeful while behaving patiently in suffering with another person is what the Lord calls us to. Can you allow someone else to cause you suffering and let them do it more than once? What about 100 times? 1,000 times? That is what a true Christian needs to be able to do is to love someone in spite of their behavior and to be extremely patient far greater than what your flesh wants to endure. I personally know that this can be done. Many will talk about putting up boundaries and one woman from Bethel Church of Redding, CA's SOZO inner healing ministry told me that I needed to set up boundaries with a person that I was married to who treated me with extreme abuse but I told her the Lord told me to take it and would not release me to share it with anyone until He allowed me to which was over six years later and that eventually He would use all that I took for His good. It is important to always seek a direct word from the Lord because just because someone puts a general guidance on a situation in a book or is a counselor does not mean it applies to every person and every situation. Everyone has a different calling and sometimes the Lord takes a person through an extreme tribulation due to their extreme anointing on their future ministry and how many lives that will be impacted. Had Joyce Meyer been rescued after the first time her father sexually abused her, do you think she would have had the anointing on her ministry that she does today which impacts lives of millions around the world? Absolutely not. Extreme trials and tribulations that are willingly endured can eventually become extreme anointings by the Lord that will affect thousands upon thousands of lives around the world when the person has finally completed their tribulation to be launched into ministry and their calling.

Galatians 6:9 "⁹ And let us not grow weary while doing good, for in due season we shall reap if we do not lose heart. ¹⁰ Therefore, as we have opportunity, let us do good to all, especially to those who are of the household of faith."

We must love others that are challenging and not give up on them. We must be very patient with them and their behavior and see them through the eyes of Christ. Do good to them, especially if they are believers. Most importantly, get a word from the Lord who will provide you with insight on your situation and then get confirmation from someone else that hears clearly from the Lord.

Proverbs 16:32 "He who is slow to anger is better than the mighty, And he who rules his spirit than he who takes a city."

You must not allow yourself to lose your control or peace when someone tries to provoke you. Look at them with the eyes and ears of Christ and if they say something that causes you to want to get upset, walk away and bind the spirits of anger from them and offense from you and just let it go. You must always keep control over your emotions at all times because once you lose it and speak out words that you regret, you give the enemy the right to hurt both you and the other person and it may take a long time to get your peace back. Just walk away and keep your peace on.

Psalms 37:7-8 "⁷ Rest in the Lord, and wait patiently for Him; Do not fret because of him who prospers in his way, Because of the man who brings wicked schemes to pass. [8] Cease from anger, and forsake wrath; Do not fret – it only causes harm."

Do not try to make your circumstances with someone change by forcing your will upon them. Wait and allow the Lord to change them in His timing and during the proper season. Yes, it will take longer than you want but during the waiting, the Lord is bringing about changes to you to make you more like Him. Do not EVER allow yourself to get in anger and do not worry or be afraid because that allows the enemy access to hurt you. Keep your peace on!

Romans 8:25 "But if we hope for what we do not see, we eagerly wait for it with perseverance."

How many of you have been hoping to live in a more serene state of peace in your life? Are you tired of striving over and over and over? Well, have hope and stop striving! Thank God for your peace and then look forward to receiving it. The Lord wants to come in and give you the peace that you are looking for but you have to do your part. Speak life and not death over your situation and thank Him for resolving it. Envision your situation being resolved and expect it. Then go for a walk or enjoy your time doing something that brings you peace and enjoyment.

Psalms 27:14 "Wait on the Lord; Be of good courage, And He shall strengthen your heart; Wait, I say, on the LORD!"

This passage is pretty straight forward. WAIT ON THE LORD!! Stay positive and be patient. Wait for the Lord to do the work that you want to see come to pass. Perhaps you are waiting for the Lord to change your spouse and see them set free from what has been torturing them since they were a young girl. Give them to the Lord and thank Him that they have been delivered and then go about living your life in freedom. Yes, you may cry on occasion as it is taking longer than you want to wait…but do not give up. Be of good courage which means be resolute – do not waver!

2 Peter 3:9 "The Lord is not slack concerning His promise, as some count slackness, but is longsuffering toward us, not willing that any should perish but that all should come to repentance."

If the Lord gives us chance after chance after chance to repent for our sins and come to Him, then should we also give others the same grace with which to make mistakes and win them over? If the Lord has tremendous patience (longsuffering) towards us then we most certainly must give people the same. Keep in mind that if a person has some very deep wounds from their father or mother, it may take most of their life until they learn how to totally forgive and cast out any spirits to get freed.

Colossians 3:12-15 "¹² Therefore, as the elect of God, holy and beloved, put on tender mercies, kindness, humility, meekness, longsuffering; ¹³ bearing with one another, and forgiving one another, if anyone has a complaint against another; even as Christ forgave you, so you also must do. ¹⁴ But above all these things put on love, which is the bond of perfection. ¹⁵ And let the peace of God rule in your hearts, to which also you were called in one body; and be thankful."

I love these verses! Bear with one another means to endure each other and not give up even when the other person may cause you to feel pain. We must forgive all that have ever hurt us and then forgive 70 x 7 times (which really means unlimited) each day. We must let God's peace rule our hearts and be thankful and never complain out of our mouths about anything.

Romans 15:5-6 "⁵ Now may the God of patience and comfort grant you to be like-minded toward one another, according to Christ Jesus, ⁶ that you may with one mind and one mouth glorify the God and Father of our Lord Jesus Christ."

These verses talk about how God's patience and comfort should cause us to want to be of the same mind toward others on earth in order to bring Him glory. We simply need to transform ourselves to becoming patient like Christ and He will be glorified and lifted up.

Psalms 103:8-10 "[8] The Lord is merciful and gracious, Slow to anger, and abounding in mercy. [9] He will not always strive with us, Nor will He keep His anger forever. [10] He has not dealt with us according to our sins, Nor punished us according to our iniquities."

God is slow to anger and long in extending us grace. He will not argue with us or stay angry forever. He wants to limit punishing us according to our sins as He wants to bless us. We can never take for granted, however, that grace means we have a license to do whatever we want. If what we do is contrary to His will, we will receive consequences for our sins so stay out of sin and stay close to God.

Joel 2:13 " So rend your heart, and not your garments; Return to the Lord your God, For He is gracious and merciful, Slow to anger, and of great kindness; And He relents from doing harm."

God wants none of His children to perish, but if we continue to sin, He has no choice but to allow our circumstances to be consequences.

James 1:2-4 "[2] My brethren, count it all joy when you fall into various trials, [3] knowing that the testing of your faith produces patience. [4] But let patience have its perfect work, that you may be perfect and complete, lacking nothing."

If any of you lack peace, if any of you have wants, if anyone is discontented, then you probably do not have patience. Be of good cheer when you have to endure a trial because your faith will be tested which will produce stronger patience and after it completes its perfect work in you, then you will be made perfect and lack nothing.

Isaiah 26:3 "You will keep him in perfect peace, Whose mind is stayed on You, Because he trusts in You"

We cannot have peace without trusting the Lord and keeping our mind on Him. We have to trust the Lord for everything and not get into fear. Trusting Him will often times mean that we have to be patient and wait.

Philippians 4:6-9 "⁶ Be anxious for nothing, but in everything by prayer and supplication, with thanksgiving, let your requests be made known to God; ⁷ and the peace of God, which surpasses all understanding, will guard your hearts and minds through Christ Jesus. ⁸ Finally, brethren, whatever things are true, whatever things are noble, whatever things are just, whatever things are pure, whatever things are lovely, whatever things are of good report, if there is any virtue and if there is anything praiseworthy – meditate on these things. ⁹ The things which you learned and received and heard and saw in me, these do, and the God of peace will be with you."

One must keep their minds on positive things that are true, noble, lovely, good reports, and virtuous and they will experience the peace of God in their lives. Be anxious for nothing, trust that the Lord has got it and then be patient until the manifestation of your requests have come to pass.

James 1:19 "¹⁹ So then, my beloved brethren, let every man be swift to hear, slow to speak, slow to wrath; ²⁰ for the wrath of man does not produce the righteousness of God"

This verse sums up what it means to walk in the Lord. Be quick to listen, slow to talk and slower to get angry because getting angry produces no righteousness of God whatsoever. You simply cannot choose to let someone get you angry in order to walk every day like you are called to by the Lord. You should never, ever be angry with anyone. As soon as you feel a spirit of anger rise up in you – choose to let it go. Speak out "I bind and rebuke you spirit of anger!" and then walk away. Pray in tongues if you have to and watch your peace come back to you. Change the old nature of your former self into the righteousness of Christ with the peace that passeth all understanding.

These are all good scriptures to remind us how we are to be very patient with people and when we do, we create an atmosphere of peace and there is much good that will come out of it. So be patient and slow to anger so that the presence of the Lord can be with you at all times.

CHAPTER 7

It May be Time to Part

Staying in peace can be especially challenging when you live with someone who is constantly in strife with you at a very high intensity. A person that controls, manipulates, criticizes, and lies on a regular basis could be hosting the Jezebel spirit due to deep father wounds from childhood that were never healed (my book *Restored to Freedom* covers this topic extensively). Living with a person who operates every day in speaking out words that hurt you over and over again, year after year wears you down and can cause you to feel extremely depressed and ultimately could develop thoughts of suicide so you must protect yourself at some point. Men are more susceptible to staying in relationship with women for longer periods of time and taking more verbal assaults due to the fact that they are men and are programmed to take anything that comes against them. I personally know men and have experience with seeing women who have physically attacked their husbands as the demonic spirit manifested in them. Women who are involved with a man that is verbally and emotionally abusive to them will especially need to protect herself against any physical attacks. They should never allow themselves to stay living in the home of anyone that physically tries to harm them. A stepson or son/daughter that was affected by another person who hurt them and now behaves every day with disrespect and words of harshness will try to make you take on their responsibility for them. So what do you do when you are constantly being hurt emotionally over and over again and are drained on a 24/7 basis?

The best thing to do when strife has escalated past the point that you can take it is to part (Pray, Assess, Return, Together). If someone is attacking you and will not relent, the best thing to do is tell them that you need to separate for the moment. The length of time for the moment may be just for ten or fifteen minutes in order to get to a place of safety, quiet, and peace again. You may just have to walk away from the person into an adjacent room or bathroom or you may need to walk from your kitchen to an upstairs or basement bedroom. If the aggressive person who is verbally attacking you wants to follow you wherever you go, you may need to run outside or get in your car and leave. I have experienced where the person tried to stop me from leaving by standing behind my car in the garage or driveway prohibiting me from leaving and chasing me into another room and that can make it especially challenging to get away. Persevere as much as you are able because as long as that person is operating out of the enemy spirit on them trying to control you, they will verbally barrage you with no relenting. It is obviously not healthy for your spirit to be around them and you need to "get out of Dodge."

PRAY. Once you are safely apart from your family member, the first thing to do is to pray. Declare out loud to come against the enemy spirit on your spouse, child, or family member. Speak out something like, "I command the enemy to be shut down, and bind and rebuke him from (name) in the name of Jesus!" and "I declare that (name) is at peace and is calm and will only speak words of love from their mouth!" Remember that even though your family member may be getting hit by the enemy, you also have an authority as a believer and can help them by going to war against the enemy for them. Ultimately, they need to get their peace back by calming down and realizing that they have been hit by the enemy and it may take them several hours to get their peace back. Understand that the same authority that you have to command healing like Jesus did is the same authority you carry over demonic forces as well. The other person does have a free will and if they continue to stay angry and speak out enemy words - it may take them much longer to come back to a calmer state. Pray for their eyes to be opened and scales removed to what the enemy is doing to them.

If you have your prayer language (and I highly recommend everyone to ask the Lord for it if they do not have it), praying in tongues will bring you back into a state of peace very quickly. Pray as long as it takes for you to be in peace which could be just five minutes or as long as thirty to keep the enemy from speaking to you. Praying in tongues is praying the perfect prayer and when you declare words out loud that are perfect, you change the atmosphere and more rapidly get your peace back and break down the enemy on and around others.

ASSESS. Assess means to determine what state of mind that your family member is in after you have prayed for them. How long do you stay apart from your loved one? The Holy Spirit can direct you as to what the state of mind that your loved one is in and if they are calm again yet. Sometimes it may only take fifteen minutes while other times it may take an hour or several hours. You may need to text the person to test the waters to see what state of mind that they are in. If they continue to text you back words of harshness or strife, you should stay away longer because the enemy is still affecting them. You can let them know that you will come back when they are calm again, so they are not afraid that you will not come back. A woman that has endured many relationships or marriages where her husband or men left her will need to be reassured that you will come back or else the enemy will whisper to them that they are going to lose another man again and their fear will escalate to try to tighten their grip over their husband. Also, if your family member tries to call you over and over in rapid succession, you will know that they are not at peace and you need to stay away longer until their behavior is consistent with being peaceful.

I knew one woman who was so scared of her father and brother that she allowed them to berate her on the phone for over an hour, blaming her for everything and making her feel more hurt and was unable to hang up and let them know she needed to go. She said that if she did not take the verbal abuse and hung up that they would call her back over and over until she answered and then really let her have it. The enemy spirit on someone can be extreme in every way imaginable but you must stand up for yourself to protect you from further harsh treatment and to come against the enemy in your family member. Eventually they will learn that they can no longer abuse you and make you do what they want and will have to treat you with respect. It may take several months or years of training them before they understand that you will not allow the control and abuse any longer.

So, the proper assessment of the status of your loved one should be taken after you have prayed and given them time to calm down into a state of peace again. Once you have determined sufficiently that they are now at peace again, you are safe to then return.

RETURN. Once you have assessed that your family member is back at peace you can return to them. When you return, you need to be careful that your family member has not lied to you only to get you to come back so they can verbally abuse you again. Return only after you are confident as much as you can be that they are now at peace again. When returning, it is best to approach them carefully because if they lied only to get you to come back so they could really let you have it again verbally, then you need to part again and you may want to stay away overnight for your own safety and to teach them how to tell the truth to you. If they are safely at peace, then stay in love towards them and never speak any words of condemnation to them or scolding. Respond to them with the love of the Father and speak only kind, loving, and gentle words that the Lord would have you say. It would be good to help them see that when they "lost it" that the enemy was behind it all and not them. They are not a "bad person" but the enemy was very bad in trying to cause strife between you. When you can consistently connect them with how the enemy gave them a thought and then they spoke it out instead of saying how you were hurt by them, they can receive it much better. When you

86

equate that they were being used by the enemy and is why they lost their peace, they can start to realize that it was true and eventually you can teach them about commanding the spirits to go from them whenever they are starting to lose their peace. If they will not receive you, then it may be time to part again because you do not want to return only to start hearing them strive again. Once they have stayed in their peace for an hour or so and can talk to you calmly, it would be good to spend a little time together in that peace.

TOGETHER. Being together after an episode of strife is a good thing because it reassures the person that you love them and want to help them stay in peace. You can spend time walking outside in nature which usually brings a person into more peace or you may just hold each other and hug them reiterating that you love them and you both must help each other to realize that it is always the enemy that causes one of you to lose your peace. After an enemy attack, it is always good to pray together and if you both have your prayer language - I would recommend praying in tongues for at least ten to fifteen minutes as this ushers in more peace unlike anything that you could do. The more that you can move back into the peaceful Spirit mode away from the flesh, the better. Praying in the Spirit shuts down the enemy from any backlash of being able to speak to your spouse or family member. Since you have been apart for a significant amount of time, you should try to spend time together enjoying something together for at least an hour or more depending on the amount of time that you were apart.

There may come a time that you simply must separate for a season from someone that is being affected by the enemy in a strong way because the enemy will try to shut you down especially if you are involved in ministry. If so, ask the Lord if you are to separate and He will confirm to you. The purpose of separation will be to help your loved one deal with the spirits that are afflicting them in order to get freed. They should work with a Holy Spirit led counselor who hears from the Lord to provide insight to them as to what has gone on in their lives and then be able to help them get delivered. You will need to stay at a safe and peaceful place in order to recover from the attacks. If the person will not admit that they have any areas to be delivered from or to work on and want to keep the spirits and thus the horrible behavior, then you need to ask the Lord what He would have you do next. You should concentrate on drawing closer to the Lord through this separation and if you are separated from your spouse, make sure to not allow the enemy to tempt you to confide closely with a person from the opposite sex that could be unhealthy in an emotional or physical sense as this could open up an entirely new issue to deal with. Stay pure before the Lord at all times.

Parting should be done as long as the person continues to be over the top when it comes to their reactions or behaviors towards you and have minimal desire to be willing to work on their issues through deliverance or Holy Spirit led counsel. The goal of it is to help train the other person that if they are going to continue to be abusive, you will not tolerate it and will leave. Over time, they usually learn to change because they grow weary of being alone and genuinely want healthy companionship. They also normally will need some deliverance of the spirits that have caused them to behave so aggressively so need to seek out a good Holy Spirit led counselor that understands how to get people free from demonic spirits.

CHAPTER 8

Love Me Forever Free

People who are hurting tend to hurt other people, and there are a lot of hurting people in this world. They were not loved unconditionally when growing up and later lash out in their pain to others who try to love them. As Christians, we are called to love others like Christ, and the Lord had me write a book called *Loving Like Christ* which explains just what the extreme love of Jesus has called us to do for others. Underneath everything, what people want is to be loved by someone unconditionally. Unfortunately, what happens is that so many people who marry come from broken families, and the enemy causes them to speak out words that hurt their loved ones due to the enemy affecting them by whispering words to them. Then, after the harmful words are spoken, walls go up; and this puts a wedge between them and the person they love. What people want is to be loved, pure and simple. What happens though is that they will hear the enemy's voice, and he causes them to control, manipulate, criticize, or otherwise hurt those who love them in an unhealthy manner that causes them to pull away.

So in order to make sure that you are able to properly love someone yourself and to be able to live in peace – you should confirm that you are indeed free from any afflicting spirits that have spoken to you and stolen your peace. How do you do this self-assessment? The easiest way to determine this is to think about what kind of thoughts usually go through your head. Do you have loving, kind, peaceful thoughts most of the time, or do you have thoughts of jealousy, control, manipulation, selfishness, harshness, anger, unhealthy sexual temptations, and then act upon those thoughts by speaking out harsh words or possibly acting out behaviors that are not good?

If you often have thoughts that are not Christ-like, then you most likely could have demonic spirits that are afflicting you that you need to be set free from. We see this all the time in my Healing Rooms as people come in who are married and are ready to divorce in order to get back to peace. I usually start out by getting a word for them from the Lord; and there is always something that hurt them when they were younger which caused them to partner with an enemy spirit or be tormented by one. Therefore, I lead them through renunciation prayers which command generational curses to be broken from them as well as Jezebel, Leviathan, and Ahab spirits. The Lord told me that the top reason for divorce is the Jezebel spirit because it causes a person to be very controlling, manipulative, deceitful, and sexually impure. Most of those that suffer from Jezebel are women due to their more tender hearts being hurt by father wounds, although I have delivered men from it as well. They receive the Jezebel spirit due to having wounds of rejection, control, and other harshness that hurt them through ways that were void of unconditional love.

Peaceful and loving thoughts should be normal but sadly are not for many people. If a person cannot stop the enemy from hitting them with negative thoughts, the only effective way to deal with the torment is to have people take their authority in Christ and command them to go. I am going to list some prayers that have been proven successful thousands of times in my Healing Rooms, over the phone, Skype sessions, Facebook Messenger video sessions, FaceTime sessions, and with people around the world that have read the prayers from my website and also through my books. On the following pages, I am going to list my prayers to break free from the torment. I'm first going to list the generational curse prayer, then prayers to break off the Leviathan spirit, which is listed in Job 41 and causes a person to have pride, twists things in their head, as well as blaming other people instead of taking responsibility. They often times have back and neck pain that never gets healed when prayed for because the spirit wraps around their spine and can also cause cancer and other debilitating diseases. Many people have the Leviathan spirit due to father wounds, but it can also come in through a father, grandfather, or other relative up their ancestry line who was involved with Freemasons, Scottish Rite, or Shriners as they have them recite prayers in private that come against things of the Lord and give right to the enemy. My book *Restored to Freedom* covers Leviathan and Jezebel in detail. Then I will list the Jezebel spirit prayer for those suffering from being controlling, manipulative, deceitful, and sexually fixated. I will also list the Ahab spirit prayer. I talk in detail about this spirit and how to get free in my book *Waking The Lion Within.*

Prayer to Break Off Generational Curses

I break all curses or vows that have ever been spoken over me from my mother and father and from all generational curses that have been spoken over anyone in my ancestry all the way back to Adam and Eve.

In Jesus Christ's name, I declare that I am not in agreement with any form of sin, or disobedience that operates in this world and against the throne of God, as I am not in agreement to any person, or family member who deliberately sinned, or perverted God's ways. In the Mighty name of Jesus Christ, I thank You, Father God, for Your good and righteous ways, and I seek to live my life by Your Spirit and reap the rewards of living by Your righteousness.

I repent for every relative connected to my family ancestry who has deliberately, or without spiritual wisdom, sinned against my Lord, or His people. I realize that all sin will be judged one day and that each one of us is accountable for what we have said, or done, but I am repenting for my family's sins in that I shall be released from any curse these sins may have produced against me. I put all of my sins and my ancestors' sins at the foot of the cross and declare that Jesus Christ has paid the price and that Father God, you have forgiven us for all.

I break all generational curses of pride, lust, perversion, rebellion, witchcraft, idolatry, poverty, sickness, infirmity, disease, rejection, fear, confusion, addiction, death, and destruction in the name and by the blood of Jesus.

I curse all traumas in my ancestors and descendants lives that have had any right to me and command all memory of these to be forever forgotten and never remembered again. I replace these traumas with peace. I speak that any and all nightmares in sleep will be turned to joy and loving dreams and visions from the Lord.

I renounce the behavior of any relative in our family background who has lived more for the world than for God. I renounce any ungodly beliefs, traditions, rituals, or customs that my people may have followed or acted upon. I repent of those family members who sought to fulfill the selfishness of their desires, and those who have perverted God's righteousness, for I myself choose to serve God and live by His ways.

I declare that my descendants will receive blessing and favor from this day forward. That we will be blessed with love, joy, and peace throughout our lives and that Jesus will be the King of our lives.

Amen.

(Now take a couple of deep breaths and you should notice that you feel more at peace).

Leviathan is depicted as having seven heads which are Pride, A Critical Spirit, Confusion (Stupor), Impatience, A Lying tongue (Deception) and Contention (Discord, Hate), Murder. These are reflected in Proverbs 6:16-19: NKJV *"These six things the Lord hates, Yes, seven are an abomination to Him: A proud look, A lying tongue, Hands that shed innocent blood, A heart that devises wicked plans, Feet that are swift in running to evil, A false witness who speaks lies, And one who sows discord among brethren."*

Below is Job 41 which describes the Leviathan Spirit:
New King James Version (NKJV)

1 "Can you draw out Leviathan with a hook,
 Or snare his tongue with a line which you lower?

2 Can you put a reed through his nose,
 Or pierce his jaw with a hook?

3 Will he make many supplications to you?
 Will he speak softly to you?

4 Will he make a covenant with you?
 Will you take him as a servant forever?

5 Will you play with him as with a bird,
 Or will you leash him for your maidens?

6 Will your companions make a banquet of him?
 Will they apportion him among the merchants?

7 *Can you fill his skin with harpoons,*
  Or his head with fishing spears?

8 *Lay your hand on him;*
  Remember the battle—
 Never do it again!

9 *Indeed, any hope of overcoming him is false;*
  Shall one not be overwhelmed at the sight of him?

10 *No one is so fierce that he would dare stir him up.*
   Who then is able to stand against Me?

11 *Who has preceded Me, that I should pay him?*
   Everything under heaven is Mine.

12 *"I will not conceal his limbs,*
   His mighty power, or his graceful proportions.

13 *Who can remove his outer coat?*
   Who can approach him with a double bridle?

14 *Who can open the doors of his face,*
   With his terrible teeth all around?

15 *His rows of scales are his pride,*
   Shut up tightly as with a seal;

16 One is so near another
   That no air can come between them;

17 They are joined one to another,
   They stick together and cannot be parted.

18 His sneezings flash forth light,
   And his eyes are like the eyelids of the morning.

19 Out of his mouth go burning lights;
   Sparks of fire shoot out.

20 Smoke goes out of his nostrils,
   As from a boiling pot and burning rushes.

21 His breath kindles coals,
   And a flame goes out of his mouth.

22 Strength dwells in his neck,
   And sorrow dances before him.

23 The folds of his flesh are joined together;
   They are firm on him and cannot be moved.

24 His heart is as hard as stone,
   Even as hard as the lower millstone.

25 *When he raises himself up, the mighty are afraid;*
   Because of his crashings they are beside themselves.

26 *Though the sword reaches him, it cannot avail;*
   Nor does spear, dart, or javelin.

27 *He regards iron as straw,*
   And bronze as rotten wood.

28 *The arrow cannot make him flee;*
   Slingstones become like stubble to him.

29 *Darts are regarded as straw;*
   He laughs at the threat of javelins.

30 *His undersides are like sharp potsherds;*
   He spreads pointed marks in the mire.

31 *He makes the deep boil like a pot;*
   He makes the sea like a pot of ointment.

32 *He leaves a shining wake behind him;*
   One would think the deep had white hair.

33 *On earth there is nothing like him,*
   Which is made without fear.

34 *He beholds every high thing;*
   He is king over all the children of pride.

Prayer to Renounce the Leviathan Spirit

Lord, I come before you with a humble and contrite spirit and command all spirits of pride to be gone from me forever in Jesus' name. I ask You, God, to remove from my life any influence from the spirit of Leviathan. I reject this spirit completely with all my heart and command it to be broken off me forever, never to return. Forgive me for any ways that I have served this spirit either intentionally or inadvertently. Forgive me for any ways in which I have been twisted or have twisted the truth, that I have listened to distortion of the truth or have distorted the truth. I devote myself to bringing unity, not division or confusion, into the church and in my personal relationships, and will therefore honor other Godly members and those you have placed in authority over me.

It states in Isaiah 27:1 *"In that day the Lord with His severe sword, great and strong, will punish Leviathan the fleeing serpent, Leviathan that twisted serpent; And He will slay the reptile that is in the sea."* I declare that Leviathan is severed from my life now and forever more. By your grace, I will speak the truth in love and dedicate myself to expressing the truth of your word in my life, and have a humble and contrite spirit in the precious name of Jesus. Amen."

I command Leviathan's head, body, and tail be completely gone from my body and send you to hell in Jesus name! I declare that my back, discs, and spine be completely aligned perfectly and any organs are untwisted and made perfect. I also speak to my legs that they are both the exact same length in Jesus name. All sickness and disease in my body be gone now and I declare every cell in my body be completely healed. Thank you Jesus!

Prayer to Renounce the Jezebel Spirit

Heavenly Father,

I come before you with a contrite, humble, and sincere heart. Thank you for having my eyes opened and scales removed today to the truth of what I have been battling in my life. I was truly a victim of my circumstances as I was an innocent child that was being controlled, manipulated, and hurt through my father (and/or mother) as they were hurt by the enemy through their parents as did their ancestors, as the pain and abuse was a vicious cycle that will now be broken over my life and all of my descendants. I am ready for this controlling spirit to be broken off of my life once and for all. Today, I take back what the enemy has stolen from me and I command all painful memories of my past to be removed forever, never to be remembered again. I forgive all that have hurt me in my past and break off all spirits of offense that I have taken. I choose to forgive my father for all that he did to hurt me. I choose to forgive my mother for all that she did to hurt me (and you should name anyone else that has hurt you as there is power and healing in forgiveness).

I cancel every negative and unscriptural word ever spoken over my life and all physical or sexual acts that have hurt me throughout my lifetime. I break the power of the spirits of confusion, fear, control, anger, deceit, pride, arrogance, and manipulation and exchange all hurts and pains from my past to be taken by Jesus Christ and forever healed and replaced with His love, joy, and peace for the remainder of my days on earth. I command all the effects from serving the spirit of Jezebel be broken off of me and my descendants forever.

I now command every demonic influence of any name from the spirit of Jezebel to be broken off of my life and I truly repent for my serving of these spirits intentionally or inadvertently. I renounce all wrong associations that I've had which served the spirit of Jezebel. I repent for all those that I have hurt with my controlling behavior and declare that I will no longer serve the powers of witchcraft from this moment forward. I declare a divorce with the spirit of Jezebel. I want nothing to do with the wickedness of that spirit in my life and declare that I will serve only the one true and living God with all of my being.

All the wounds that Jesus took for me on the cross were sufficient for me to be healed forever and I exchange my broken heart for a new heart that is soft, gentle, loving, pure, and strong (symbolically pull a knife out of your old heart and replace your heart with a new one from your heavenly Papa who loves you unconditionally).

I declare that I will serve Jesus Christ and His Word with all of my heart from this moment forward. I declare I will not compromise my living to any standard below Christ's love, purity, and Holiness. Thank you, Jesus, for healing my broken heart forevermore and giving me a new life to serve you with.

In Jesus blessed name. Amen!

(Next, just rest and take a deep breath with your new clean heart and receive the peace from your loving Papa Father. You should feel the weight of the world lifted from your shoulders and feel a tremendous peace like you may have never felt before. There is power in your words, and life and death are in the power of your tongue.)

Prayer to Renounce the Spirit of Ahab

Father in Heaven, I come to You in the name of Jesus Christ, my Savior and Lord. Father, it is my desire to see Your Kingdom come into my life and into my marriage (or future marriage), and my family in a new and powerful way. Right now, I make the decision to forgive any and everyone who has had influence in my life to cause me to be less than the person of God You wanted me to be. Father, I forgive the following persons who have unfairly controlled me (name anyone who comes to mind).

I repent of being like an Ahab and ask You to forgive me. I now take back the authority and responsibility You have given to me that I relinquished to Jezebel. By the power that works in me according to Your strength and anointing, I will watch over and minister to my new husband or wife in Christ and my children. Father, I ask for wisdom and guidance as I do this.

In the Name of Jesus, I break every curse that has come upon me or been spoken over me and my family because of the influence of the Spirit of Jezebel within my husband or wife and any sins of ours or our ancestors. I command every evil spirit that has come in through curses that I or others have spoken over me to leave me. Go out of me, now, in the name of Jesus Christ! You must also loose my (husband or wife) and family. I say to you evil spirits, GO! I declare that I am bold in the Lord and command restoration of everything that the Spirit of Jezebel has done to hurt me. I am blessed and highly favored and am strong in the Lord and decree that my future life will be far greater than my former. As a believer in Jesus Christ, I have been granted the same authority as Christ and declare divine health throughout every cell in my body. I have the mind of Christ! I will help others that I know to become free from every Spirit of Jezebel and Spirit of Ahab, and decree that I will have a strong anointing over those spirits the rest of my life.

Thank You Father for deliverance and healing, now and in the days to come. I Praise Your Holy Name. AMEN!

CHAPTER 9

I Will Never Strive

2 Timothy 2:23-26 KJV "²³ But foolish and unlearned questions avoid, knowing that they do gender strifes. ²⁴ And the servant of the Lord must not strive; but be gentle unto all men, apt to teach, patient, ²⁵ In meekness instructing those that oppose themselves; if God peradventure will give them repentance to the acknowledging of the truth; ²⁶ And that they may recover themselves out of the snare of the devil, who are taken captive by him at his will."

I also like the Message version of the Bible because it explains the language in much easier to understand words that cannot be confused.

2 Timothy 2:22-26 Message "Run away from infantile indulgence. Run after mature righteousness – faith, love, peace – joining those who are in honest and serious prayer before God. Refuse

to get involved in inane discussions; they always end up in fights. God's servant must not be argumentative, but a gentle listener and a teacher who keeps cool, working firmly but patiently with those who refuse to obey. You never know how or when God might sober them up with a change of heart and a turning to the truth, enabling them to escape the Devil's trap, where they are caught and held captive, forced to run his errands."

If we are a true Christian, then we should NEVER EVER strive with ANYONE at ANYTIME! So this chapter will hopefully be able to drive home the point to all that read it that if you choose to engage in strife - you will pay a price for it. You simply cannot avoid it. Often times, one person is getting hit with the enemy's thoughts and then when that person opens their mouth and spews it over you, you cannot take offense and spew it back or else you will be in a lot of strife that you cannot get out of it for a while.

John 14:27, "Peace I leave with you, My peace I give to you; not as the world gives do I give to you. Let not your heart be troubled, neither let it be afraid."

We are called as Christians to live in peace with everyone (even ourselves) and never to strive. So what exactly does strife or striving mean? It means angry or bitter disagreement over fundamental issues; conflict, friction, discord, dissension, dispute, quarreling, wrangling, bickering, controversy, etc. Does strife always mean that you have a conflict with another person, or can you also strive with just yourself? Let me explain.

I had never had any knowledge of what striving really was until my mentor Chuck from Southern California had talked to me about it at length. He said that striving meant anything that causes a person to become uncomfortable in any way either with another person or with yourself. When I first heard that statement, it was a new concept for me to ponder. It was like a revelation because I never thought about that before, yet it made a lot of sense to me. Here are some examples.

Let's say that you are having a lovely dinner with your handsome husband on the island of Maui in Hawaii at sunset. You've both eaten your salads and started on your mahi-mahi and vegetables. You get a thought about your step-children out of the blue that causes you to be in fear about what they may be doing to your home when you are gone. So you just mention it to your husband who you know will not be happy if you put his children down or speak about them in a negative light. Now the mood has changed from perfect bliss to offense and anger. The night has been ruined, all because the enemy gave you a thought of fear (false evidence appearing real). This is strife. Had you captured the thought right away and commanded the fear to go in Jesus' name, then you would have remained in peace and never spoken it out loud to your husband. He would not have been hurt by you when you put his children down and he would then not have spoken a negative word back to you. So the enemy won and you both lost.

Another example; a man is working hard at his job and trying to make as much money as he can to allow his wife and children to be able to afford nice things. He gets a thought that he may get downsized because the company sold off a division that half of his time was spent working with. He then gets into fear and has trouble sleeping at night worrying about what could possibly happen to him. He started to fixate on thinking about how things would be horrible if he lost his job, and a day later he snapped at his children much more strongly than he normally would have. His wife then jumped on him for being so short with their children, and then he retaliated towards her and they were angry with each other and did not get intimate for several weeks causing him to slip into pornography to satisfy his sexual needs. She then learned about it and told her friends about him, and they all said he was not able to be trusted and she should divorce him. It all started because of a thought from the enemy about possibly losing his job – which never materialized because they reassigned him to another division three weeks later. So the enemy won and strife was created with fear. Then he lost his peace, she lost her peace, and now their children are in fear due to a possible divorce, so their grades at school are falling and they are no longer going to church. Their children's friends have changed, and they are all hurting and not healthy. Can you see the downward spiral that can happen when you lose your peace and get into strife?

Facebook. Ahh...something that can be so beautiful and encouraging and relational yet at the same time be horrible and devastating to people. I know some people who abhor Facebook like it is some kind of evil thing (as well as other social media like Twitter, Instagram, Periscope, etc.). It can be used for good or it can be used for very bad, just like words that are spoken out by people in everyday life. I choose to use them for good and to help encourage people and share what the Lord is doing in my ministry and personal life. I communicate to thousands of people around the world and even use Facebook's video technology to do ministry counseling sessions worldwide. I also make people aware of new books the Lord has inspired me to write to help more people become restored to freedom in Him. Some people, however, hear more from the enemy and use it in ways that are devastating to others. If a person hears from the enemy strongly, they will type out words of lies, expose sins, violate confidences, crucify family and friends, and cause all those that read or watch them to feel slimed. So many strive constantly on Facebook about everything, and a person would be wise to either not read or watch what they constantly post or just unfriend or block them altogether. Cyberbullying is a term that no one talked about when I was a youngster in the early 1970's. Today, it is very common and can literally cause a person to commit suicide due to reading about words that were completely false and unfounded, but another person who was used by the enemy decided to make it appear true. Accept your friends wisely and if a certain person is causing you to feel uncomfortable or lose your peace – then feel free to "just say no".

Here is a common example for far too many people. You are driving down the highway on a beautiful, sunny afternoon. The speed limit is 60 mph but you like to drive 70 mph. You are in the fast passing lane and come upon cars that are both going about 60 mph in front of you in both lanes. You slow down and wait for a few seconds to see if the car in front of you will speed up to pass the slower car but they do not. You feel frustrated and become irritated at the slower car and speed up to get closer to them. After just five seconds, you begin to get irritated and start honking at the car to move over. The man driving the car that you just honked at gets angry with you. He speeds up but then slows down on purpose to irritate you because you honked at him trying to make him move over. Road rage ensues for both of you. You both start to drive erratically and before you know it, a policeman drives up behind you and pulls you over. When you park your car - he charges you with a $250 ticket for road rage and unsafe driving. This is called striving. Had you just been patient and not gotten frustrated or angry, the person would have eventually moved over, and you would have been able to go about your merry way. Instead, the enemy told you that this person was purposefully going slow to irritate you. You took an offense and got mad at them and now you must pay $250 for your impatience!

Striving is also when you are trying to make something happen on your own strength. Let's say that you desperately want your ministry to grow so you call churches and try to get them to have you speak. You send out email after email and call pastors and try to convince them to allow you to share your testimony and do ministry. You try to get on Christian TV and radio shows to promote your new book or CDs, and no one wants to have you on. You plead and call your best friend who knows someone that is in the Christian music business and knows someone that is in a larger ministry, but to no avail. You try to connect with someone who knows someone that knows someone who has connections to a nationwide ministry but again, that falls apart. Then, there is the Lord's way where He opens the doors that no man can open. He connects you supernaturally to other people in ministry who the Lord lays on their hearts to connect with you. The Lord will promote you without you having to connect yourself in due season at the appointed time, and then all will know that the Lord's hand is upon you. That is what is called 'divine favor' and is the proper way in which your ministry should flow. Those who strive for man's favor will be short lived, while those that allow God's favor to take over will see amazing things happen in their lives and ministries.

Let's say that your 18 year old daughter is completely disrespectful to you and behaves very selfishly. She tells you that she is going to date a boy that you do not want her to date. You become angry and infuriated because of her defiance to your authority and tell her "no" but she defies you all the more and walks out. You then threaten her that if she goes, she will not be allowed to come back home to live with you. She moves in with her boyfriend and you "disown" her and don't talk to her for months. A year later, she gets pregnant and has an abortion and your heart is broken, but you still want to show her "tough love" because someone told you that was how you should handle that situation so you do not talk to her. Then the enemy tells her that "you did not want her anymore" and she has nowhere to turn, so commits suicide and now you have to attend her funeral, and feel guilty and condemned for the rest of your life. Had you checked yourself at the point that your daughter told you she was going out with her guy friend, instead of threatening and telling her she would be disowned, you would have stated that "I wish you would not go out with this boy because I feel he may ultimately cause you to get into some things that will hurt you" and kept your relationship intact, then she would have returned to you that evening and you could have had a loving and civil conversation instead. Unfortunately, the enemy whispered to you to "not take it" from your disrespectful daughter, and you listened and took the bait and now you have no daughter as the enemy won. These things happen every day and the Lord is saying it is time to wake up to the tactics of the enemy. It is time to love like Christ so that the enemy will lose. Too many parents get into a power struggle with their children and try to force them to do what they want and then end up breaking their relationships, sometimes forever.

What if you have a stepson and all he can talk about is sports and complains about how miserable his life is. You would like to help him see things from a spiritual perspective and tell him he needs to stop complaining and to learn how a Christian should behave. He believes he knows everything and that you know nothing even though you are always at peace and a cheerful person while he is like Eeyore from Winnie the Pooh and every day gets worse than the previous one. The enemy would like to whisper to you to say something about God, and the Bible and point out where he is incorrect. If you do that, he will get mad at you, feel condemned, and lash out verbally, causing him to withdraw and not talk to you for a week or longer and hold a grudge against you. Therefore, since he cannot have a discussion about spiritual things, you need to shut your mouth, show discernment and wisdom, and only talk with him about sports for now. If you try to convince him of spiritual things, it will only lead to strife and the Lord will not be pleased with you for starting an argument because you know better as you are more mature in the Lord than he is currently. Even though your stepson is wrong in his spiritual beliefs, you simply cannot "go there" (talk about) with him about spiritual things because it will only lead to strife. That is showing your Christian maturity and wisdom in the Lord, and allows you to keep your peace on.

Another example in marriage; what if your wife has a strong spirit on her which controls everything and will escalate a discussion into strong, verbal, angry words if she does not get her way. First of all, it is very wearisome on her husband if he has had to endure that for many years. Realizing that she is this way, he has most likely had to give in over and over and over again. Let's say that there is a decision that needs to be made about where to eat. She cannot stand to eat at fast food places, but you have several other children that are involved in the decision of where to eat after church and you have just a short amount of time to eat because you have to go to her son's softball game. If you know that she cannot stand to eat at Burger King, although everyone else involved would have no issue with it, but you suggest eating at Burger King anyway - you know that she will go ballistic with you. This is called strife and unfortunately, you were the one that started it. Even though everyone else would have been fine with eating there, you knew that your wife absolutely hated to eat there and it would cause her to speak out words of anger. Yes this seems like a trivial thing but unfortunately, sometimes we have to sacrifice for someone else who has issues with various things.

What if you have a friend that is scared to death of ever eating anything warmed up in a microwave because he had read that it could lead to cancer or some other diseases. If you purposefully chose to warm up his food in a microwave instead of an oven, then you are striving with him because you know that he will have a challenge with eating it. Conversely, if you want to eat healthy food (fresh fruits, veggies, non-fried foods, no doughnuts, etc.) and your friend wants to go to watch a college football game with you and loves to eat brats, hotdogs, wings, French fries, cookies and doughnuts, and you tell him that you will not eat that food because it is not healthy – then you are striving with him because he does not think that there is anything wrong with the food. You know that health wise, it won't be good for you or your stomach but on his behalf, should you partake so as not to cause him to take an offense against you or be hurt that you are rejecting him for just this one time that he considers special? What if your brother believes meat is wrong because an animal had to lose its life and you choose to eat meat purposefully in front of him? 1 Corinthians 8:12-13 NKJV says "[12] But when you thus sin against the brethren, and wound their weak conscience, you sin against Christ. [13] Therefore, if food makes my brother stumble, I will never again eat meat, lest I make my brother stumble." Also in 1 Corinthians 8:8-9 NKJV it states "[8] But food does not commend us to God; for neither if we eat are we the better, nor if we do not eat are we the worse. [9] But beware lest somehow this liberty of yours become a stumbling block to those who are weak." Then there is Romans 14:21 NKJV "It is good neither to eat meat nor drink wine nor do anything by which your brother stumbles or is offended or is made weak." Therefore, you need to be very cognizant of how people react when you are eating. One man made fun of his sister-in-law at Thanksgiving because his mother had to make gluten free macaroni and cheese for her because she said she was allergic to gluten. Her brother-in-law hurt her and she snapped back at him and they almost broke out into major strife which would have ruined Thanksgiving. Christians need to be aware and gentle with others that have concerns with various foods. The enemy is everywhere trying to cause strife however he can.

Family reunions and holidays are always an interesting time of angst for many. Why? Because people in families host enemy spirits whom people have seen operate in them for their entire lives and anticipate that strife will continue to pour out of the same people as they have done year after year before. I have literally seen some children who grew up with harsh or excessively rule-based parents who had strong religious spirits and forced their children to do everything they said. They tried to be perfect for them but when they became teenagers, they completely turned to the dark side because they felt no love from their parents and were tired of being scolded and corrected their entire lives. Some relatives are known for "speaking their minds" which can often be interpreted as – saying words out loud that the enemy whispers to them that they are thinking in order to inflict pain on someone else. Anyone know of someone like that in their family? Aren't they such fun to be around and you just cannot wait to connect with? Not. What generally happens is that people will avoid them, if possible. What about the relative that likes to brag about all they are doing or how much money they are making? Again, many of the relatives will try to avoid them because they can cause people to feel jealous and less than. Does anyone know people who tell you about all of their pains, sicknesses, and diseases? Now there's a fun conversation to listen to for hours. Then there are those who love to dominate conversations and make it all about them, so they will usually look to connect with a timid person who is polite and will listen for hours while not interrupting them. That way they can talk on and on and on. Meanwhile, the timid person starts to fall asleep until they get shoved to wake up because the dominate person is still not done talking. After everyone leaves, they all talk about each other and say how glad they are that they don't have to go through that mess again until the next holiday or family reunion. Of course, if you are one of the fortunate souls who grew up with all godly people who genuinely love everyone like Christ, you would have healthy conversations talking about exciting things the Lord is doing for you with no jealousy or strife. That, of course, would only account for about 1% of the families in the world.

Can it be considered striving if someone who is stronger in the Lord says something to someone weaker in the Lord that causes them to get angry even though the person who spoke it out first was completely right in what they were saying? Absolutely! Say that you speak to someone who is weaker in the Lord than you about having sex with someone outside of marriage. What if they are behaving that way out of the pain in their lives looking for someone to love them desperately and then you tell them, "You are sinning by having sex with someone you are not married to." Or, "you are living with a person you are not married to and will go to hell if you were to die tonight." That is strife because the other person will not be able to handle what you said because they are not mature in Christ. You must cover everything in love and know what space that person is in who is sinning. You need to discern that they are acting out of their pain and can only receive a very light level of ministry and possibly no correction whatsoever, until you have built a solid relationship with them. It may take a person who has been hurt their whole life several years to be able to handle more spiritual truths or correction. It is a journey and we as Christians need to discern and be patient with all that we minister to.

Think about all the people who hold up signs on the streets that state "Gays are all going to hell!" Do you think that makes a person who is suffering from enemy spirits want to actually change as they feel more condemnation? I don't think so. One time I went with others from my church to a gay pride festival in Indianapolis, under the guise of doing "dream interpretations" and appearing somewhat like "New Age" in order to draw in hurting people. A young man who was gay came into our tent and told me that he had a reoccurring dream that he was "on a boat in the middle of the ocean with no sail and was just being blown here and there by the winds." The Lord gave me the interpretation immediately. I shared with the young man the following, "You were hurt by someone in your younger years (The

111

Lord shared with me that he was molested when he was younger and then his family did not know how to help command the spirits out of him so he got tempted into the gay lifestyle and his family then turned their back on him). You had plans to go into ministry, but once you were hurt - you lost all direction and now have been drifting here and there and feel like you are being tossed about in the waves of life with no real love." He started crying and then opened up that he was molested when he was younger. He was planning to become a pastor but then drifted away from his family. People that were gay showed him some type of love that drew him into their "family" while his true family disowned him and wanted nothing to do with him anymore. Now he had no direction in his life. He began crying and I hugged him and told him Jesus loved him and that He was sorry for all the pain of rejection from his religious family. It was a moment that I will never forget because the young man needed approval from a godly man and to trust that the Lord still loved him and was calling him back through His unconditional love. We must be discerning when we speak words to a person that they cannot receive and must always cover it in love from the Father. Too many so called "Christians" are condemning, harsh, judgmental and religious, thinking their sins are somehow better than someone else who sins differently. They are nothing more than a modern-day Pharisee which disgusts the Lord. Loving like Christ involves seeing others who have been hurt in extreme ways by looking through the eyes of Christ and having compassion for their pain.

What about complaining about something? How did that work out for the Israelites in the desert after escaping from slavery? They had to wander in a hot desert for 40 years until all the complainers died off and then the Lord took the new generation of non-complainers into their Promised Land. I know so many Christians that spew out negative words of misery to anyone that will listen and everyone feels like they have been slimed as their spirits feel heavy and broken after listening to all the junk. The Greek word translated 'complainer' literally means "one who is discontented with his lot in life." It is similar to the word grumbler. Complaining is definitely not a fruit of the Spirit and is damaging to trying to stay in peace, joy, and have patience which comes from the Spirit. Complaining is destructive and debilitating personally, and only serves to make our witness as a Christian to the world non-existent. Would you be attracted to

112

someone whose religion espouses grumbling and complaining about their life and others? Not me. I know it is hard when you have been hurt and are currently miserable in your walk, to not look at your circumstances and speak it out of your mouth but you simply must not speak a word of grievance out loud because that gives the enemy the upper hand and right to keep making your life sad and depressing.

Who was the first complainer on earth? Adam. After he and Eve disobeyed God, he told Him "that woman you put here with me – she gave me some fruit from the tree, and I ate it" Genesis 3:12. Then he got booted out of the Garden of Eden for his prize. Had he apologized and manned up for his part – perhaps the Lord would have treated him a little differently, but he totally blamed his wife for it instead of admitting that he made a mistake.

Adam's son Cain also complained, although mainly within himself. Genesis 4:6-7 NKJV "⁶ So the Lord said to Cain, 'Why are you angry? And why has your countenance fallen? ⁷ If you do well, will you not be accepted? And if you do not do well, sin lies at the door. And its desire is for you, but you should rule over it." We also know that Moses complained (when you are the leader of over a million Israelites who are all complaining to you, about you, and about God – well, it's somewhat understandable, albeit not right). But to Moses' credit, he even cried out to God on behalf of the complaining Israelites to save their lives. David complained. Job complained, but was able to sanctify his complaints which took humility.

Clearly as believers, we are challenged not to complain. Philippians 2:14-15 NKJV "¹⁴ Do all things without complaining and disputing, ¹⁵ that you may become blameless and harmless, children of God without fault in the midst of a crooked and perverse generation, among whom you shine as lights in the world…"

When we complain, we move ourselves from the heavenly realm to Satan's realm in the earth. We change from a spirit of peace to a spirit of depression and negativity. We move onto enemy territory and eventually do not even like our own selves. The Lord cannot move on our behalf when all we do is speak negative words. A complaining spirit leads to fighting and quarreling because complaints lead to envy and strife which is at the root of many problems. All of this is called striving and as we previously read at the beginning of this chapter – a servant of the Lord must not strive. The less we complain, the more that God can move for us on our behalf to accomplish what we are so desperate to see manifest in the physical!

CHAPTER 10

Walking Out Your Peace

My life was changed forever when I began to learn in 2009 about walking in peace and trying to stay out of strife – especially in the middle of a relational hurricane which I had experienced the previous ten years that would increase ten-fold the following six years. When you take a step back to see others the way Christ sees them, and consider yourself to be an ambassador for the Lord on earth and that you are here to serve and love on others that are hurting, then you can extend them grace because they are not as far along in their Christian walk as they need to be - just like you were not when you first started. Am I still growing in my Christian walk every day? Absolutely, every day, month, and year we should all continue to be getting fine-tuned by the Lord and become more like Christ every day.

So what practical tools can we use every day to ensure that we are becoming more like Christ and walking in His peace so that when we enter the presence of someone else that they can feel the love, joy, and peace that exudes from our spirits? People can tangibly feel the spirit of peace on you if you are walking in it, and they will usually calm down when they are around you. Have you ever been around a person who is very anxious or fearful? It will get on you and you will want to run from them because you can feel your anxiety level get stronger in your chest. I have felt it and it is not enjoyable at all as I wanted to just run away so I could escape back into my state of peace. How do we stay in peace the majority of the day and actually start to live in peace every moment of the day, week, and month? Listed on the next pages are practical things that you can do to bring in more peace than you have ever seen before in your life:

1) **Spend time to get to know the Lord.** He wants a personal relationship with you and will give you direction and words of wisdom as much as you want as long as you are sensitive to the Holy Spirit. I have regular "conversations" in my mind throughout the day with the Lord and it is so special that I would never go back to the old dead way of living with no relationship with the Creator of the universe. There is something special about asking the Lord a question or asking for insight about a certain matter and then hearing from Him and knowing that the choice you are making is the right one. When you walk every day conversing with the Lord and know that He wants to talk with you, there is nothing like it in the world. If you have never heard Him speak to you before and would like to hear Him, just get quiet and ask him to speak to you and then listen for what you hear in your mind. His voice sounds like your own but usually speaks words or concepts that you would not come up with on your own. When the Lord told me that I would love a woman that I had just met 2 weeks prior 'like Christ loved the church' back in early 2009 - I would never have thought of that on my own. I knew it was not the enemy's voice and so it had to be the Lord's. Spending time with the Lord can also be just getting quiet and sensing what the Holy Spirit is directing you to do. I will often write down significant words in my journal so that I can refer back

to them in the future to remind me of what the Lord promised me. Also, if you wake up in the middle of the night, you should be at your greatest peace and can usually hear very clearly from Him what He wants you to know. Reading His Word is also a good thing but not if you are approaching it as a religious tradition just to be reading thinking that will make you godly. Also, if you read too many chapters, you have the potential problem of not actually getting all that you are reading into your spirit. It is better to read a few verses and fully comprehend them then to read several chapters and totally forget what it was all about. You may also want to keep a journal every day and write down thoughts that you have throughout the day to be more cognizant of when the enemy tries to speak to you causing you to lose your peace. You can keep track on your smart phone and whenever you notice a thought that is from the enemy, rebuke it and command it to go. As you become more aware of the voice of the Lord versus the enemy or even your own thoughts, you will be able to more quickly shut the enemy's voice down and all the lies he tries to speak to you.

2) **Receive your prayer language and pray in tongues often.**
For those that are reading this book and do not have their prayer language (tongues), I would highly recommend that you ask the Lord for that gift because there is such power in praying in tongues. If you do not have your prayer language yet and want it, just get quiet before the Lord or put on some praise music and start speaking out whatever comes through your spirit, not your mind. Some people only have one or two syllables when they first start trying to pray in tongues so just go with it and start speaking out. One lady could only say "M&M" and kept saying that for almost two weeks. Finally, she received her whole prayer language and it overwhelmed her as she was driving down the road as the presence of the Lord was so strong all over her. If it sounds strange at first just continue to press in and over time - it will develop into an amazing prayer language that will take you places you have never been. There is so much of His power that develops in you and is released when you pray in tongues for an hour or

more a day. The enemy cannot speak to you when you pray in tongues to cause you fear or anxiety so if you hear a lot of enemy thoughts throughout the day, just start praying in tongues. You will experience a peace and a power to which nothing else compares. You are also prophesying your future when you speak in tongues which allows the Lord's destiny for your life to move forward. Start your morning off with praying in the Spirit and watch what starts to happen in your life as the worries of the day will not hit you as you will feel the Lord's presence and peace all around you. Throughout your day, continue to pray in the Spirit and you will feel such an amazing presence around you as you transition to becoming more powerful in the Spirit which is who you really are in Christ.

3) **Trust in the Lord with all your heart.** Typically the Lord takes His people through a season of having to trust Him to meet their needs instead of providing for themselves in order to make them stronger against the enemy's future tactics. In other words, when I used to make a lot of money in my financial services technology position, I did not need to trust in the Lord for my finances as I had accumulated over half a million dollars and was making well over six figures and could buy whatever I wanted. In order to get me to draw closer to Him and have total reliance and trust in Him to be my provider and be in peace at all times, I went through a season for several years of total dependence on the Lord to meet my financial needs. My heart was to come into my own ministry, so I needed to transition from trusting in the world's ways and receiving money from my job which was my way, and instead into the Kingdom's ways and trusting that the Lord would provide for me, however He would provide. If you want to become more like Christ and come into a stronger level of peace, then you have to learn to start living the way He did with total trust that all of His needs would be met. You will, often times, need to experience some circumstances that may not feel pleasant for a season, but eventually it causes you to change to become who you really are in Christ – and it makes you stronger and your anointing on your life grows with it. As

I went from week to week with having no extra money and no way to make more than what He would allow me to make, it slowly changed me into being able to trust Him for everything. I had to depend on Him because I simply could not change my circumstances. When I owed $75,000 in credit cards and had no job, I was finally able to get myself into peace as I trusted the Lord to provide for all my needs because there was no way that I could change my circumstances. The Lord wanted me to be in that space for a season until I was comfortable and at peace that He was my total provider, and I would never get into fear. Then I saw Him start providing for more of my financial needs week after week through donations that came into my ministry. I started to see more favor and more connections coming to me to grow my ministry so that I had absolutely no fears whatsoever, that if I had no regular money source coming in to me, that still He would somehow provide for me without me having to strive to make it happen because I was not going to ask or beg anyone for money. He kept providing for me in a myriad of ways every week, and I stayed in peace more and more knowing that He would provide for all my needs as more people kept coming to me for ministry services from around the world. Trusting in the Lord builds your peace as you can eventually never get into fear whether it is for finances, health, relationally, career or ministry, anything. It is such a freeing position to be in when you know that He will provide for all your needs like Paul wrote about in Philippians 4:19 NKJV "And my god shall supply all your need according to His riches in glory by Christ Jesus."

4) **Walk away from strife.** What do you do if you happen to live with a spouse or child or other person that spews out words of strife the majority of time that you're living with them? It can be very challenging to live life day to day because the aggressor is right in your face and there is nowhere to run and hide. You need to minimize the interaction time that you have with those persons by either moving to a different room in the home, or going for a walk outside of the home, or driving away for an hour or so, because your spirit can only take so much striving before it feels like you are being overloaded. When

you tell your aggressor that you need to leave, make sure you handle the departure as wisely as possible. In other words, if you are leaving a controlling spouse, you may need to be very gentle and tell them you need to get something at the store, so they will more readily accept your leaving. Remember that you are dealing with a spirit that is on them and you have to be smarter than they are in order to leave without them trying to keep you there. Also, if someone wants to engage with you in a topic that you know will start strife (they have an instigating spirit) and are trying to pull you in to an argument, you may need to tell them "we need to talk about something else" or just change the subject so that it does not generate strife. Walking away from someone that wants to engage in strife can be very challenging if you do not use wisdom and discernment so ask the Holy Spirit to give you guidance and He will. Just say no to striving at all times and you will live in more peace

5) **Spend time around nature.** When you are trying to stay in peace, there are few substitutes for being in nature. Whether it is just going for a walk around your block or neighborhood or if you are able to walk by a small pond, creek, river or lake, something happens when you're able to hear or see birds, stare at peaceful water, look at the mountains or valleys, and commune with the Lord. You can just feel the presence of the Lord and His associated peace within when you are outside in a scenic setting. If you are located in a large city, it can be more challenging to feel the peace of nature because you may have to drive to a park and even then, you will probably still be able to hear cars and trucks. What did Jesus do when He wanted to get away and listen to His Father? He headed for the mountains to rejuvenate to be in more peace. It may be good to just get away for a weekend and head to a state park and rent a cabin and just enjoy your time with the Lord.

6) **Do activities that you enjoy that bring you peace.** To stay in peace, do things that you enjoy that are good and fun for you. Perhaps reading books (spiritual and non-spiritual),

120

watching sports, exercise activities such as aerobics, lifting weights, playing squash, racquetball or tennis, swimming, running, taking bike rides, roller blading, etc. will be good exercise for you while at the same time - reducing your stress levels which produces more peace. It could be just going out with friends and chatting over a meal that would be fun for you, provided they are friends that do not provoke and cause strife. Movies (albeit, wholesome ones) could also allow you to be at peace for a couple of hours although society has really limited many of the choices unless it is a Christian movie. Playing cards with friends, attending Christian worship nights, music in the park, cookouts, and anything that is wholesome fun can recharge you. When you are doing the fun activities, let your brain rest and do not think about anything heavy or serious. You may even want to think about taking a mini vacation somewhere not too far away.

7) **Limiting the amount of activities in your schedule to an amount you can handle.** So many people over-schedule activities in their calendar so that they end up having no free time to just do nothing and rest in peace. We all are blessed with 24 hours in a day and some of us waste our time away producing nothing with the time that we are allotted while others work themselves to sickness and exhaustion. Sometimes you need to just schedule time to do nothing and rest in peace. I am as guilty as anyone as I recently was working 40 hours plus a week and then every Saturday ministered in my Healing Rooms leaving my home at 10:00 am and not getting back home until around 6:00 pm. I had ministered in my Healing Rooms every Saturday since October of 2015 (only took off three Saturdays in the first twelve months as the ministry was growing). I also recently started attending three church services every Sunday at three different churches at 9:00 am, 10:30 am, and 2:00 pm. I was also busy writing five books in seven months during 2016 when I was not working or ministering. I understand that we all have seasons of busyness and ministry, but we cannot keep that pace up all the time for the long haul or we will just wear out and crash. Prioritize times of doing nothing so that you

can just rest in the Lord's peace because even Jesus got away from the crowds and headed for the mountains where He could spend time resting in peace and hearing His Father.

8) **Read your Bible because you want to read it and not because you feel condemned to read it.** You should desire to read the Word because you want to actually grow and become more mature and not because you know it is the right thing to do. You will want to read it because it becomes alive and more exciting to you and the Holy Spirit will help you see things that you never knew before. Ask the Lord for your spiritual eyes to be open and watch what happens. You will be able to comprehend and understand Scriptures like never before (and if you are struggling to stay awake when reading or struggling to understand it, then you most likely are being influenced by the Leviathan spirit and need to read the renunciation prayer that I included in Chapter 7. You can learn much more about it in my book *Restored to Freedom.*). Many may have grown up reading the King James Version of the Bible, which is much more challenging to understand because of all the "thees" and "thous," so I would recommend that you read a version that is easier to understand. My personal preference is the New King James Version, but I also enjoy the Amplified and even the Message for further easier explanation in a different way. Read the Word because you want to and not because you feel you have to. Also, many times reading fewer verses is more impactful then reading many chapters. You want to get the Word into your Spirit and not just read and forget what you read.

9) **Limit your exposure to people who strive.** Obviously, there are people in your life who will strive until they are set free (and if ever) from the enemy in their life. As you grow stronger in the Lord, you will be able to more easily handle being around the people that strive because you will have discernment and also not take an offense from the words they speak out. Until you get to that higher maturity level in Christ, you need to stay away from the people that will cause you to

be hurt. One woman was hurt by the words her controlling and manipulative father said so had to stay away from him for several years in order to try to limit her pain from hearing the words he would speak and at the same time teach him that he could no longer just call her up and speak horrible words to hurt her. The same woman had a younger brother who also would berate her on the phone and she could not just hang up on him because then he would call back and really let her have it. The spirits on people will cause them to do some very hurtful things. Sometimes you may have to avoid seeing someone that you love by waiting for several years due to the words they speak out which hurt you. This can be very hard if the people are your mother or father, but you need to protect your heart. So be wise and stay away from the unhealthy people as much as you can in order to bring about your healing from the damage that they can bring on you.

10) **Spend time with healthy people in the Lord.** Gravitate towards spending as much time with people that are healthy in the Lord, who will not speak out words to cause you pain. Be very selective because some people are wolves in sheep's clothing and they may appear to have your best interest at heart while actually having an agenda that causes them to be elevated and to use you for their own selfish gain. You need to especially be aware of those that operate in the Jezebel spirit. Those people had significant father wounds from rejection and control that were never healed, causing them to partner with a voice that promises to protect them which ultimately is extremely adept at being seductive to pull you in to trust them while leveraging you for positioning them in more power over people. They are master liars that would serve well in the CIA or KGB or being an undercover agent. The simple test is to ask a person if their relationship with their father was healthy and loving or if it was harsh and controlling or if they felt rejected. Unless they have been set free, they could be very subtly controlling and it is very hard to tell. Ask the Holy Spirit to give you a high level of discernment to determine if the person is healthy or not and then confirm it. Unfortunately, there are far more people in the world that have

been hurt and never healed, thus they operate out of their wounded pain instead of being able to help heal. Healthy people heal people while hurting people hurt people. In the church, there are many well-meaning people that truly have a calling on their life to help people, but they are still wounded and are not able to help others in effective ways and sometimes hurt them because they do not understand the spiritual component that a person needs deliverance from for true peace and contentment. I have seen some counselors at churches that are not Holy Spirit led who cause more damage telling people what to do based on their own wounded hearts that were never healed. Many counselors and pastors get into their profession because they were hurt in their lives and want to help others but until they have gotten completely healed and clean from any demonic spirits that may be operating covertly in them (i.e. Jezebel / Leviathan), they could actually cause you to feel more condemned or direct you in ways that are not what the Lord would have you do. Pray that the Lord will bring good people into your life and command the people that are sent by the enemy to be gone from your life.

When you are walking in the peace that passeth all understanding on a daily basis, there is nothing in the world that can take away your peace. When you trust the Lord every day of your life to provide you with protection, provision, and divine health, then that leads you to a perfect peace that the enemy cannot take away. When you have no fear that the enemy will hurt you and you know who you are in Christ, you can then walk in His full power and authority and experience peace every day of your life. There is no amount of money in the world that can replace peace and, in most cases, the more money people have, the less peace they will have. Getting to your peace is one journey while staying in peace all the time is the prize worth obtaining. It is possible to keep your peace on every day but only if you transform your mind of the past into the mind of Christ and walk in His ways all the days of your life. Love you!

REFERENCES

The New King James Version of the Bible
The Message Version of the Bible
The King James Version of the Bible

Final Thoughts

Keeping your peace on is a must when you are trying to become more like Christ. Striving is where many of us have been for the majority of our lives and the Lord wants to transition us into a more peaceful state. When you walk every day in the Lord's peace, you are able to bring true love, joy, and peace into the lives of a hurting world. The enemy should have no part in your life and when he sees that you are no longer affected by your circumstances, he will have to try some other tactic which will not be as affective. Show, by example, that you are like Christ by bringing your peace with you wherever you go.

If you would like me to speak and minister at your church, seminar, or conference - you may contact me on my website. If the revelations in this book have helped you and changed your life or saved your marriage, you may wish to make a tax deductible donation to Restored to Freedom at http://www.restoredtofreedom.com which will help continue to get the message out to people all over the world that there is hope and a way to gain total freedom in Jesus Christ. Amen.

NOTES

NOTES

NOTES

NOTES